NARROW GAUGE IN THE ROCKIES

Of the three narrow gauge railroads built north out of Silverton like the fingers of a hand into the Uncompaghre Mountains by Otto Mears, the Silverton Railroad with eighteen miles of track was considerably the longest. Locomotives and rolling stock, including Mears's celebrated combination restaurant and sleeping car with its abundant menus and opulent wine card, was interchangeable and ran over the Silverton Northern and the Silverton, Gladstone & Northerly as well as the Silverton itself. Of all the short lines in the record the Silverton was among the most profitable, its diminutive coaches and combines usually being filled to capacity at a flat twenty cents the passenger mile. The Silverton was also famous for the passes variously in buckskin, silver and gold which Mears presented to shippers and public citizens of importance. The carrier maintained the only narrow gauge housed-in turntable in the West. Here No. 100, running extra, is shown in a painting by the distinguished artist Howard Fogg, with its diminutive train along the margin of Mineral Creek. The year is 1888 and Otto Mears's affairs are at their zenith.

By Lucius Beebe & Charles Clegg

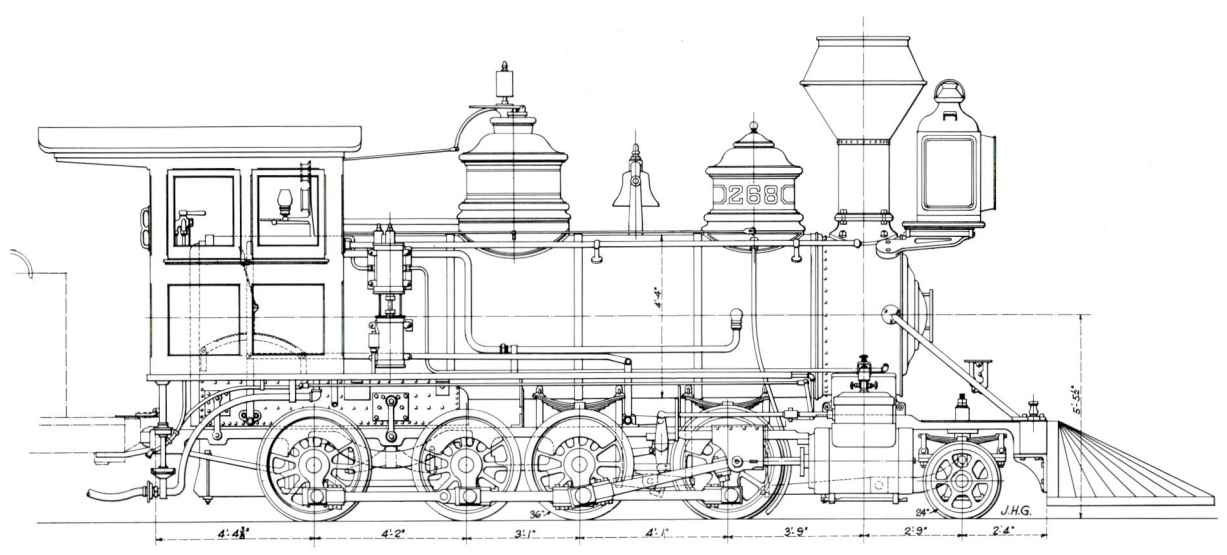

NARROW GAUGE IN THE ROCKIES

HH
Heimburger House Publishing Company
7236 W. Madison Street
Forest Park, IL 60130

Published by Heimburger House Publishing Company,
Forest Park, Illinois.
Copyright©1993 by Ann Clegg Holloway
All rights reserved. Nothing may be reprinted or copied in any manner, in whole or part, without the express written permission from the Publisher. Printed in the United States of America.

**Heimburger House Publishing Company
7236 W. Madison Street
Forest Park, IL 60130**

Library of Congress Catalog Card Number: 93-78312
ISBN: 0-911581-28-6

Acknowledgments

For signal assistance in the preparation of this book the authors are indebted to Mrs. Alys Freeze and the staff of the Western Collection of the Denver Public Library and to Miss Ina Aulls, now retired from the librarian's office there, to Richard Kindig, Jackson Thode and Ed Haley for multiple good offices including the reading of the manuscript copy of this book, and for pictures and photographs to the Colorado State Historical Society, A. M. Camp, Otto C. Perry, Richard B. Jackson, Gerald Best, John W. Maxwell, Robert W. Richardson, Edgar T. Meade, Jr., Fred Jukes, Otto Kuhler, James M. Morley, Cal Wall, O. K. Peck, Captain Frederic Shaw, Carlton T. Sills, Jim Shaughnessy, Robert Richards, E. Preston Calvert of Pullman Standard, Robert Hale, Carl Fallburg, Morris Abbott, Arthur D. Dubin, Gilbert Kneiss, Muriel Wolle, and finally to Howard Fogg who, better perhaps than any contemporary painter, seems to the authors of this book to comprehend at once the glory of steam and the wistfulness of the narrow gauge.

OTTO PERRY

Dedication

To the Many Gracious Individuals Who Helped With the Gift of Pictures, their Time and Criticism to Make This Book Possible, But Especially to The Members of the Rocky Mountain Railroad Club and the Staff of the Denver Public Library Western Collection, Its Pages Are Dedicated In Gratitude and Appreciation.

OTTO KUHLER

Contents

Denver & Rio Grande	12
The Mears Short Lines	94
Denver, South Park & Pacific	122
Florence and Cripple Creek	166
Uintah	176
Rio Grande Southern	190

Foreword

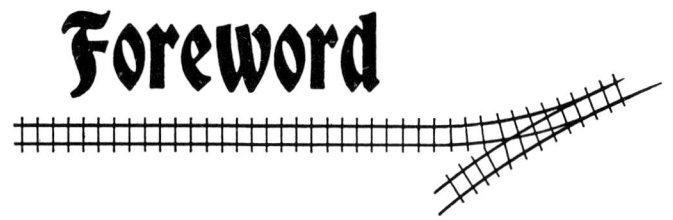

Writing of the neighboring state of Wyoming, Hamilton Basso, the distinguished historian, once remarked that "nowhere on earth has mankind in passing left fewer traces of his going".

Handily adjacent to the wastelands of Wyoming, it is difficult to imagine a place where there are more abundant traces of mankind's wistful only yesterdays than Colorado. Yet it seems probable that the marks of man in the high passes and upland parks of the Rocky Mountains are somewhat less permanent than those of Dr. Schliemann's several cities of Troy or the Mayan remains of Yucatan. The false fronts of once populous mining camps are good for a decade or so of Colorado winters at the most. The tailings and mine dumps are only a little more lasting and a few centuries will have eroded them past discerning to the most perceptive archeologists. The elemental earth is quick to reclaim the cuts and fills of vanished railroads. Thus, while for a brief period the tangible souvenirs of yesterday are at every hand, their impermanence is there also, implicit in the very nature of the society and its economics that mined the hillsides for precious metals. A rags-to-riches social emergence was not notably aware of mortality. It didn't build for the ages.

Thus the obligation lies heavily and urgent upon the historian who would chronicle the white man's first coming to the Shining Mountains and the life he brought to them. He must be nimble, as has been Muriel Wolle, to sketch and photograph the sagging facades and rotting wooden sidewalks of a hundred crumbling mining camps. He must preserve and cherish the fragile wet plate negatives from the ponderous camera of William Henry Jackson. The artifacts and possessions of the pioneers must be collated and burnished and sheltered in vaults and museums as an obligation to generations to come. The custody of only yesterday is a mortmain of responsibility demanding faithful discharge before the traces of yesterday itself vanish forever in the mutations of time.

Geologic time moved slowly in the Rocky Mountain region. The first white men, the Spanish *conquistadores* who evolved the Santa Fe trade moved but little faster. Things accelerated a little when the French took over the trade in beaver plews in the name of the Rocky Mountain Fur Company, the American Fur Company and the independents who, in a day of untrammelled individualism were very independent indeed. Neither to the Spaniards nor to the French were the Indians any more important than they were to the ultimate Yankees who succeeded both. They supplied slaves for the Spaniards and shooting galleries for the Long Hunters and the Mountain Men. The gulf that separated the white man from the Indian could be measured in the fact that the miserable Indians ate their corn. The enlightened white men distilled it into whisky with which they exalted their own personalities, poisoned the miserable Indians and provided an effective lubricant for the progress of something that was shortly to emerge on the American consciousness called Manifest Destiny.

Whisky, allied to the gunpowder of Lammot du Pont from Wilmington, was the first important agency in the white man's conquest of the Shining Mountains. Then came the coefficient of expansion of heated water translated into the fact of the steam locomotive engine. By the time whisky was being brought in on the steamcars and was aiding in the still further extension of the railroads themselves, the cutoff valve of progress was operating at its most efficient set.

Like its neighboring state of Nevada, Colorado might well have incorporated a railroad train in the heraldic economy of its great seal, for wealth, social emergence, statehood itself and the identity that has come to be Colorado all rode behind the flanged wheel cleaving to the iron rail of its primeval railroads.

In the steamcars American genius had perfected an agency of transport so incomparably superior to anything that had gone before or has since followed after as to be a way of life in itself. And of this way of life the narrow gauge was a microcosm in endearing diminutive. Its ensmalled proportions laid a compulsive hold on the human imagining and the cars carried in their strong rooms and locked express compartments the emotional treasure of a westering people. The surveyors pointed their transits and the chains followed up the long canyons and across the parks not only to Leadville and Gunnison, Telluride and Ouray. The surveys led into the ramparts and high passes of the Shining Mountains of the heart, perhaps if the Manitou spoke truly, to the very edge of the world over which the soul would one day plunge to peace forever.

When they drank at Clear Creek and from Animas, the grading gangs partook of the American sacrament, for once having tasted the rivers of fulfillment they must always return to the west that is the mystical apotheosis of American experience. Like the Long Hunters before them they took the sacrament and they turned their eyes to the sunset as they drank.

But if the men who built the railroads perceived the cloudy trophies to which they aspired at all, they were for the most part obscured by the more immediate realities of tangible things. The grades were laid along the river courses and on shelves above the abyss almost without exception toward what everyone earnestly hoped might be limitless deposits of carbonate ores if not actually free gold and silver lacking only the imprimatur of the eagle to make them spending money.

And where the stub switches were spiked to sidings and water tanks arose in the shadow of the remotest peaks there came into being the shabby romantic communities that were the mining West composed of false fronts and plank sidewalks with wooden awnings before a multiplicity of gorgeous saloons, gambling premises and brothels that boasted crystal chandeliers and rosewood pianos from far-off New York. If the cinema has accomplished nothing else, it has made a belated generation conscious of the look and sound and texture of the Old West as no other agency could serve to do it, the long mahogany bars, the ruffle-fronted gamblers, the splendid barroom nudes in bank vault frames of purest gold, the derringers, and the madames in fringes, flounces and feathers beyond all tally.

These and a thousand other properties now perfumed with nostalgia rode in aboard the narrow gauge cars and with them rode the remarkable anthology of people who lived among them, hard rock miners, nabobs, drummers for whisky firms, speculators in bonanza shares, soiled doves, Irish bartenders, Cousin Jack powder men, swampers from County Mayo and metallurgists from Harvard. Minnie the Gambler and Madame Moustache adjusted their voluminous skirts to the velvet seats of the steamcars. John Morrisey, Tom Walsh, tough old Charlie Boettcher, Spencer Penrose and Bert Carlton tossed their Gladstones in the insufficient but ornamental baggage racks and made the Golden Journey to Samarcand which was locally known as Silverton or Red Mountain or Cripple Creek. They arrived variously in jack boots or striped trousers and cutaways as their primal station dictated, but one and all they departed to drink with kings and emperors and presidents and have sons-in-law from the Almanach de Gotha. Colorado mines and the narrow gauges that served them were to evolve a generation of wealth and authority as well defined as the aristocrats of Tidewater Virginia or the China merchants of Beacon Hill. Their vestigial traces can be found in Colorado Springs and the Brown in Denver to this day, and without the three-foot ore cars that ran to the Camp Bird Mine at Ouray, Leopold, the old bearded King of the Belgians, would never have had so many mistresses or central heating in his palace at Brussels.

Practitioners of beautiful letters for some centuries now have been mistaken as to the most compulsive theme available to literature and history. It isn't true love consummated, but sudden and preferably undeserved riches that make the heart of the reader beat fastest of all. Wealth isn't just an aspect of American philosophy; it is a universal fact that has obtained since the goldsmiths first hammered out spending money in the Street of the Egibis in Babylon. And money in beautiful bucketsful was what Colorado produced with the assistance of the narrow gauges for a full half century of the Western epic.

Gold and silver were the choicest words in the lexicon of almost two generations in the Centennial State and found their way readily into its geography at Silverton, Silver Plume, Auraria, Gold Hill, Argentine, Argo, Oro City, Placerville, Carbonate Hill, Chloride, La Plata, Montezuma, Silver Coin and Treasure Hill. As evidence that chicane was not unknown among the hoisting works, there was also the Gold Brick Mining District, and precious metals even became given names as witness Silver Dollar Tabor, perhaps an extreme case.

Sudden contrast was the theme song of the diggings; sourdough and Taos Lightning today, chefs from Delmonico's and magnums of Mumm's tomorrow.

Where only last winter the wretched Utes had cowered before the tempest clad in the skins of wild animals now stood a hundred Vendomes, Windsors, Clarendons, Hotels de Paris, Teller Houses and Grand Hotels in gaudy profusion of Mansard roofs, mahogany bedroom sets, diamond dust mirrors and tesselated marble floors from the quarries of Italy. Gowns by Worth and jewels from Tiffany adorned female figures which only a brief season since had been performing like Borgias, poisoning their menfolk over cast iron cookstoves in Pickhandle Gulch. Horace Tabor with a diamond in his shirtfront that had belonged to Isabella of Spain. The Unsinkable Mrs. Brown, heroine of the *Titanic* and widow of Leadville Johnny who used their first half million dollars as kindling for the fire on a winter morning on Fryer Hill.

Thus it will be seen that the most opulent sarabands and lushest folkways, all the properties that made nineteenth century Colorado an envy and wonderment to less fortunate parts of the world, took passage in one way or another aboard the steamcars, most of them riding rails laid just three feet apart.

To perpetuate the memory of the narrow gauges a generation that would gladly exchange the comforts of here and now for yesterday in Boreas Pass has taken steps that stand as a testament of devotion without parallel among other antiquarians no matter how dedicated. The Rocky Mountain Railroad Club tells their story in volumes that only a tolerably strong man may heft; there is a Narrow Gauge Museum and Motel at Alamosa toward which dedicated railroad buffs everywhere turn their faces as Moslems toward Mecca; there is a periodical devoted solely to narrow gauge tidings which is the devotional reading of The Faithful, and there are narrow gauge books, pamphlets, post cards, excursions, engine models, book ends, beer mugs, paperweights and pictured likenesses of the cars beyond all counting. To have ridden the *San Juan* or the Silverton Train is a greater experience than to have seen Shelley plain. The Faithful sigh for the snowsheds of Lizard Head and by the waters of Gunnison they sat them down and wept.

This book will make no attempt to carry as its lading the spacious and moving legend of Colorado yesterdays, for no narrow gauge engine is possessed of sufficient tonnage rating to take it up the grade. Its concern is with the steamcars themselves and their occasional integration to the folklore of the places where they ran. The sounds of their exhaust and bells were good sounds in the symphony of Western landfaring; the freight they carried more glittering than the plate fleet of Spain. Mostly the iron ponies are now stabled forever amidst fields of asphodel and beyond the margin of Acheron. Their recollection is a gentle one, cherished in the hearts of many men. Lonely are the meadows of Middle Park and white the snows under the night winds at Telluride, for the past is there. And the great blaze of memory for a golden time.

Virginia City   LUCIUS BEEBE
1958   CHARLES CLEGG

OTTO PERRY

Denver & Rio Grande

The Long Hunters and the Mountain Men left scant trace of their going on the face of the Colorado earth. The routes they followed in trapping beaver and assembling for spring rendezvous were not dictated by grade advantage nor directness so much as by semi-military necessity, and their pack trains, except where they converge in density upon such points of distribution as Bent's Fort on the Arkansas, left no scars upon the mountainsides. A few years after the end of the fur trade, even these primeval reminders of the white man's passing were gone.

But in 1859, there occurred an event that was to alter the entire face of the region covered by the shining Mountains. The presence of gold in appreciable quantities was established in the Gregory Diggings near the later site of Central City and Black Hawk on Clear Creek, and Colorado entered a cycle of prosperity deriving from precious metals that has endured in certain aspects to the immediate here and now. There had been gold rushes into Colorado Territory before and "Pike's Peak Or Bust" had become part of the national lexicon of the fifties, but until the Gregory Diggings, the gold recovered had been ephemeral and thousands of embittered prospectors had retreated to Missouri and other border regions to lick their wounds and curse the promoters of false hopes.

Now, however, in June of 1859, there arrived from the East a party of distinguished journalists representing the most influential press of the nation and including among their number Henry Villard of the *Cincinnati Commercial Enquirer*, A. D. Richardson of the *Boston Journal*, and Uncle Horace Greely, proprietor of the venerated *New York Tribune*.

Greeley, already a figure in the national consciousness partly compounded of fun, partly of shrewdness, who cherished political delusions of imposing grandeur, was on one of his periodic tours of the West and wanted his readers to know the truth about the Colorado bonanzas. What he and his associates discovered was to set the nation by the ears. All were frankly impressed by the recoveries which, with their own unbiased eyes, they were able to witness at Clear Creek, and the three of them then and there signed their names to the celebrated report which Colonel William N. Byers promptly published in a special edition that is now a collector's item of consequence of his *Rocky Mountain News*. As fast as the magnetic telegraph could carry the intelligence to the East, it was reprinted under banner heads in Boston, Washington, New York and other metropolitan centers and Colorado was launched, under impeccable auspices, on a long and spectacular career of riches. That Greeley, who was himself possessed of an agrarian philosophy, was to have no part in the bonanzas and is recalled today in Colorado for the agricultural community that bears his name is merely ironical.

Almost immediately it became apparent that while the Mountain Men had been able to pack out their plews by muleback, no such primitive agency was going to sustain the multiplicity of gold camps which sprang up along the Rampart Range and later in the inaccessible interior of the territory. Wheeled vehicles alone could carry in the supplies demanded by the diggings, flour, bacon, raimant, whisky, blasting powder and mining tools, and only wagons could bring out the ore until such time as smelters and reducing mills could be constructed handy to the source of wealth itself.

To accommodate the vast wains and their commerce, a network of toll roads, laboriously built to a semblance of passability by human labor, came into being, the greater number of them converging upon Denver City, as the Cherry Creek Diggings was now coming to be known. A primeval toll road was opened in 1860 by Castro & Sheppard to connect Denver with Central City, and others followed throughout the state: the Denver, Auraria & Colorado Wagon Road Co., the Denver & South Park Staging Co., the Tarryall & Arkansas River Wagon Road Co., the Alpine & South Park Toll Road Co., the Apex & Gregory Wagon Road Co., the Colorado & Pacific Wagon, Telegraph & Railroad Co. The last of these was organized in 1861, nearly a decade before the first steam locomotive was to turn a wheel in Colorado, but already forethoughtful men were incorporating the railroad in their plans for the future and there was the inclusion of the magic word "Pacific" which was to be part of the title of every respectable railroad promotion for half a century to come. The names of many men associated in the location, construction and operation of these turnpikes were to become the fabric of Colorado legend: Henry M. Teller, Horace Tabor, William A. H. Loveland, John Evans, Captain Edward L. Berthoud, Richard Lacy Wootton, Jim Bridger, William H. Russell, David H. Moffat and Otto Mears.

The Colorado sixties seethed with railroad excitements, most of which were in some way associated with the location of the Union Pacific and its parallel carrier a hundred miles to the South, the Kansas Pacific. Prime contenders for the honor of being the state capital were Denver City and Golden, the gateway and entrepôt to the Clear Creek mining region. In an attempt to shorten its transcontinental route to the Pacific, the Central Overland, California & Pike's Peak Express Company in 1861 had surveyed a wagon road by way of the pass discovered at an elevation of 11,300 feet a few miles west of Central City by Captain Berthoud and Jim Bridger, and it was hoped that the Pacific Railroad could be induced to drive its location stakes through Golden, up Clear Creek and thence via Berthoud Pass to Salt Lake. But the grade was far in excess of the maximum of 116 feet per mile set by Congress and General Grenville M. Dodge's grading crew were soon throwing dirt through Cheyenne and over Sherman Hill a full 100 miles from either Denver or Golden. At the same time news, erroneously as it happened, came to hand that the Kansas Pacific was about to be abandoned for lack of funds, and Denver merchants started hastily packing Gladstone bags and hanging up iron shutters on their places of business. Everyone, or almost everyone, took a dim view of Colorado's future economy and was going elsewhere as fast as the Concord stages of Russell, Majors & Waddell could carry them.

But despite the gloom which permeated Denver business circles and could be dispelled only by the consumption of immoderate quantities of Taos Lightning in the Elephant Corral and the Community's other leading saloons, all was not lost. A connecting link, to be financed with local capital was organized by Governor John Evans between Denver and the Union Pacific's mainline at Cheyenne, and in June of 1870, Colorado found itself joined to the outer world by rail when the first train rolled grandly into its southern terminal with Chicago papers only three days old and day-before-yesterday's editions from Omaha. The confusion, glory, municipal alcoholism and patriotic oratory which were the identifying marks of railroad celebrations everywhere in the land were met in the inaugural ceremonies of the Denver Pacific Railway. The messenger of good will entrusted with a solid silver spike as the gift of the miners of Georgetown with which to spike the ultimate length of rail to the final tie failed of his trust. The faltering feet of Mercury became entangled among the cuspidors of the Last Chance Saloon & Gambling Hall, a progressive rival of the Elephant Corral, and the ceremonial moment found Governor Evans, spike maul in hand but with no spike to drive. The state's ready-witted attorney general, Sam Brown, quickly fashioned a silver spike with tinfoil gathered around a conventional iron artifact and thousands, or at least hundreds, cheered as the bearded old governor, his silk hat at a raffish angle, secured the iron and tie in bonded conjunction. The silver spike from Georgetown was later discovered in a local pawnshop, where its custodian had deposited it against funds for further jollification, and it was redeemed by Governor Evans.

L. H. Eicholtz, chief engineer for the project, was presented with "an elegant gold watch in token of his energy and gentlemanly bearing". The arrival of the first train of two "elegant passenger cars" and a baggage drawn by No. 30 was acclaimed by the joyous citizenry and the *Cheyenne Leader's* enthusiasm knew no bounds in describing the cars as "the most beautiful and elegant we have ever seen. The lady's coaches are furnished inside with Hungarian ash and black walnut set in elegant panels, showing the natural grains of these beautiful woods. The doors are finished with rosewood. Between each window is a small oval mirror surmounted with elaborate carved designs. The seats are lined with fine silk plush, the front of a beautiful Solferino color, and the backs of a rich green. The seats are the most luxurious we ever occupied, equal to a stuffed Elizabeth chair. The entire interior is of unsurpassed beauty and magnificence."

Nobody reading these transports of delight could for a moment doubt that railroading in Colorado was off to an auspicious, even an elegant start. They couldn't have been more right.

The Denver & Rio Grande Railway of General William Jackson Palmer's dreaming and the concern of this brief chronicle was in actual fact the fifth railroad to operate within the confines of Colorado. Following hard on the heels of the Denver Pacific, the Kansas Pacific at length achieved its Denver terminal in August of 1870, while a purely intrastate project, the Colorado Central, whose ranking patron was William Loveland of the "Golden-For-Capital" faction, shortly built something less than fifteen miles of track between Golden and Jersey Junction on the Denver Pacific. Another strictly Colorado carrier was the Boulder Valley Railroad, organized and maintained by Governor Evans to insure a supply of cheap Colorado fuel coal for the locomotives of the Denver Pacific and the Kansas Pacific.

The locomotives of four railroads, all of them standard gauge, were sending clouds of smoke skyward against a backdrop of the Front Range before there appeared on the scene the carrier which possessed an authentic rendezvous with history, the three-foot gauge Denver & Rio Grande.

The agency of the coming of the Rio Grande and, with it, intimations of the industrial facade and pattern which were to characterize the economy of the entire state of Colorado for years to come, was a red-headed, scrapple-eating Philadelphian of precise, if not hilarious, philosophy, who had served his railroading apprenticeship with John Edgar Thompson on the Pennsylvania Railroad and, after a brilliant military career in the Union forces, had been appointed chief construction engineer of the Kansas Pacific. General Palmer was possessed of an austere personality, reinforced in respectability by an education in England where he had witnessed the great battle of railroad gauges, a truly epic difference of opinion between the two foremost engineers of the age, George Stephenson, champion of the narrow gauge, and Isambard Kingdom Brunel, builder of the Great Western Railroad of England and an Achilles in the camp of broad gauge thinkers. In England, the broad gauge was seven foot wide, and the narrow gauge, which was eventually to become standard gauge, four foot, eight and a half inches. Further evidence of Palmer's frosty admiration of things English was his Colorado Springs home which was modeled, with modifications, after the home of the Duke of Marlborough.

Colorado Springs was one day to be known throughout the West as "Little Lunnon" because of the concentration there of wealthy British health seekers, titled remittance men and retired colonels. With the aid of William Bell, a former London merchant of means, Palmer floated a million dollar bond issue to inaugurate his railroad: $700,000 in England and $300,000 back in his native Philadelphia.

To promoters of such limited means, narrow gauge construction had an almost irresistible allure. Construction costs of three-foot rights of way, trestles, tunnels and the like were about half those of standard operations. The road's first engine, the *Montezuma,* weighed only twenty tons and rolling stock was so light in proportion that when a windstorm hit the Rio Grande yards at Palmer Lake halfway between Denver and Colorado Springs, an entire train, engine, tender and coaches, was hilariously blown off the track and required the united efforts of a section gang and a team of oxen to regain the rails.

In addition to being influenced by these material considerations, General Palmer, according to a durable Colorado legend, inclined toward the diminutive cars of the narrow gauge for moral reasons. The universal practice of the time was to sell space for not one but two occupants of the lower berths of sleeping cars of conventional dimensions. Travelers unknown to each other, or of only the most casual passing acquaintance, might be berthed in a single bed. Worse, gentlemen might be assigned to sleep in offensive proximity with persons of less elevated station. This arrangement on any railroad General Palmer might build was unthinkable and the narrow gauge solved all problems. It was impossible for more than a single occupant to occupy a narrow gauge berth.

Besides offering these inducements, social and economic, the narrow gauge was in actual fact eminently qualified for the routes eventually followed by the ever expanding rails of the Denver & Rio Grande Railway. Steep grades, narrow canyons and mountain fastnesses impervious to standard gauge save at ruinous cost were easily available to twenty-ton locomotives and coaches only thirty-three feet long. All over America the cult of the narrow gauge was laying powerful hold on the thinking of engineers and bankers alike. When the first shovelful of dirt was turned at ground-breaking ceremonies of the Rio Grande in 1870, an orator was so carried away by the vision of forty-pound rails reaching just three feet apart to the limitless horizons of time and space that he ventured the forecast that: "In twenty years a standard gauge railroad will be as much a curiosity as the three-foot gauge is today." He was in step with much of the advanced thinking of his time.

The Denver & Rio Grande Railway was chartered as the state's first narrow gauge carrier on October 27, 1870, and its mainline to Colorado Springs, a distance of 76 miles, was opened for business precisely a year from that date. During the previous twelve months of construction, the road had purchased two locomotives, one of them the *Montezuma*, a 2-4-0 outshopped by Matthias Baldwin and hailed in the builder's catalogue of the time as the first narrow gauge passenger engine to have been built by this celebrated firm. "The boom towns of Colorado were delighted beyond compare when the *Montezuma* appeared on the scene," said Baldwin's publicity department smugly. The first passenger operation over the Rio Grande's three-foot iron was in the nature of a trial run and covered four miles with two baggage cars, two smokers, and the coaches *Denver* and *El Paso* behind locomotive No. 2, the *Tabi-Wachi*.

The names of the two passenger coaches were symbolic of General Palmer's ambitions, for his charter provided for the building of 850 miles of road between Denver City and El Paso on the Texas-Mexican border, after which it was projected to continue another 900 miles to Mexico City when, if, and as suitable concessions could be obtained from whatever Mexican government might be in office when the railhead reached the Rio Grande of its corporate title. Had its thirty-five pound rails ever gotten that far, it could reasonably have expected Porfirian liberality with American enterprise to have assisted it on its way, but the contingency never arose.

From these pastoral beginnings, the Rio Grande by 1884 was operating more than 1,600 miles of narrow gauge track and had established what was generally felt to be a continental dimension by reaching out far past the Rocky Mountains and across the Utah border to Salt Lake City and eventually Ogden.

General Palmer's little giant got under way with a whoop and a holler, and in three years the population of the General's pet real estate promotion at Colorado Springs had been enlarged from a handful of squatters and destitute Utes to a tidy 2,500 more substantial residents. When the iron reached Pueblo, soon to be the setting for the puissant Colorado Fuel & Iron Company, the population of that community on the Arkansas promptly doubled. Traffic along the north and south axis created by the Rio Grande was brisk and the General and his engineers came to Trinidad, whence it would take off over the mountains to the high plains of New Mexico, without premonition of disaster.

That two major railroad systems, each with transcontinental aspirations, should, in the one hundred and second year of the Republic, engage in a melodramatic physical hassle, with overtones of cloak-and-dagger intrigue over a right of way, is a revealing commentary on the state of the frontier. The West was still the West, and the derby hats, the cord binders, and the smoking chimneys that so outraged Frederick Remington were still below the horizon. Incidentally, Remington was wrong about the derby hat as a symbol of urbanity. The hat that won the West was, in fact, not the Stetson of Remington's admiration, but the cast iron bowler which was the occupational attire of lumberjacks, railroad engineers, stage drivers, bartenders, peace officers, Wells Fargo agents, and whisky drummers past all counting. It appears, if evidence were needed, in ten photographs of the Old West to every one of plainsmen or cow poke in a sombrero.

But no matter.

The low pass to New Mexico and, indeed, the only practicable pass for the establishment of a railroad grade was the Raton up the Purgatoire, the "Picketwire" of the Mountain Men, a few miles out of today's Trinidad. A toll road had been built through the hills by Richard Lacy Wootton, who had purchased the right of way from Lucien Maxwell, each of them Mountain Men of fantastic stature in the legend of the fur trade. Wootton was somebody to reckon with. He had served with honor as scout in the War with Mexico and drifted to Bent's Fort on the Arkansas with Kit Carson, scalping innumerable Indians along the way for fun. His most celebrated exploit was the driving of 9,000 head of sheep a thousand miles from Taos to the Sacramento Valley in California through hostile Indian country with the loss of a trifling hundred head in all that perilous *jornada*. His enthusiasm for killing Indians was only matched by his mammoth capacity for the wine of the country, a cheap Mexican whisky called Taos Lightning, of which it was said that nobody with a taste for it ever lived to become an addict. Uncle Dick was an exception. He had set up shop as proprietor of Denver City's first saloon and general store, and made money in pots despite his being his own best customer. But a generous nature and the fascinations of rondo coolo and three-card monte at the Elephant Corral or the rival Progressive, run by Ed Chase, got most of his earnings. Chase lived to be Denver's foremost gambler and was fond of recalling the old days and Uncle Dick Wootton for the benefit of such celebrities as Eugene Field, Oscar Wilde and the Duke of Marlborough.

So, in much the same manner that graying codgers today buy a motel against their old age, Wootton had bought the toll road across the Pass of the Rat. He had also built a substantial adobe which combined the best features of toll house, ranch and saloon. There was a vast bar and the flow of Taos Lightning matched the flow of the Picketwire out by the back door.

So now the Atchison, Topeka & Santa Fe Railroad of silk-hatted Cyrus K. Holliday, building out of Kansas, and the Denver & Rio Grande Railway of General William Jackson Palmer arrived at one and the same time on the doorstep of Raton, gateway to the high plains and strait portal to all the Southwest of the American continent. It was a moment in history.

Neither of the contestants for the right of way through the hills was anxious to come out of his corner. They eyed each other suspiciously and spies sought out the countryside under cover of darkness. Furtive figures who might be agents for either side rode up the draws, and coded telegrams kept the wires hot out of

Pueblo on a twenty-four-hour basis. That the Rio Grande and Santa Fe had each broken the other's code only made it more interesting. The Santa Fe's President, Thomas Nickerson, and a group of directors came out from Boston and discussed the impasse in Commonwealth Avenue accents. Uncle Dick sat tight and made no commitments to either side, but his evenings were observed to be spent increasingly in the company of a reputed Basque sheepherder, whose long black serape and slouch hat gave him the appearance of a conspirator out of Drury Lane melodrama. The muffled stranger could match Uncle Dick drink for drink and he had an added accomplishment; he could play tunes on a yaller-backed fiddle that delighted the old gentlemen. The two of them sat in the bar together until all hours, sometimes doing a brief fandango with the mozos, wagon teamsters in the Santa Fe trade and other low and relaxed folk who hung out in Wootton's adobe.

General Palmer's high moral tone, on the contrary, included the demon rum along with the implications of double berths as an agency of evil, and he extended this view by imperial fiat to his staff of engineers and land-seers. A few years later he was to embrace gambling as a viper, and used his influence as the reigning power in Colorado Springs to oppose, but not beyond all evasion, the plan of Count James Pourtales for a splendid gaming casino where the Broadmoor Hotel stands today. Just now the General's prejudice extended to Uncle Dick's adobe, which was shunned as a plague spot by the Rio Grande's retainers.

Ironically, the Demon Rum was to be the deciding factor in the occupation of Raton Pass.

At long last, through intercepted telegraphic messages, the Santa Fe cohorts learned that the Rio Grande was about to move and had indeed recruited grading gangs at Pueblo which were already, in dead of night, en route for Trinidad. In the barroom of Uncle Dick's adobe, the basque fiddler came out of his disguise and identified himself as Ray Morley, advance agent, land-seer and grading engineer of the Atchison, Topeka & Santa Fe. Could his railroad secure the right to go over Uncle Dick's cherished toll road?

It must have cost the old man some heartbreak, for the Santa Fe teaming was his sole source of income, but apparently Morley squared things on a satisfactory basis. A handful of regulars from the bar moved out into the 4 a.m. darkness of the Raton with a single lantern, Morley's knowledge of the well-scouted terrain, and a gallon jug of Taos Lightning for courage. They were half an hour ahead of General Palmer's chainmen and shovel gang and the pass was theirs.

When, a few months later, the first Santa Fe engine rolled up the grade and headed out into the high plains of New Mexico, it was named *Uncle Dick*.

Obviously this debacle put an end to General Palmer's dream of a narrow gauge empire that should overflow into Mexico and he returned from a metaphorical Moscow a wiser if not notably chastened promoter of railroad properties.

Already Palmer may have sensed that the true destinies of the Rio Grande lay not to the South but in the West, and that a change in direction might change the railroad's run of luck. Even before the head-in with the Santa Fe, tidings had come of inland deposits of low grade but easily available coal at Durango in the San Juan basin, and a narrow gauge mainline had taken off at Walsenburg for what was eventually to be Alamosa on the Rio Grande River on the far side of the towering Sange de Cristo Range. The line, which included the celebrated Muleshoe Bend (narrow gauge version, of course, of horseshoe) and plunged from Veta Pass, towering 9,339 feet into the cobalt Colorado sky, down to Alamosa and Fort Garland, is a lasting memorial to the road's chief engineer, J. R. De Remer. La

Veta was then the highest railway pass in the entire world. All along the way, the Rio Grande promoted townsites and made a little money with which to push its reluctant iron over another mountain range or up another valley.

Eventually, over what is to this day one of the most awesomely spectacular examples of mountain railroading in North America, although freight alone now traverses its rails, the little trains came to the company town of Durango. The next few decades saw this remote and lonely community on the Rio de Las Animas Perdidas become the veritable world center of narrow gauge railroading. But of this more in its appropriate place.

Its triumphant snatching of the Raton and the golden destinies its possession implied had gone to the Santa Fe's head. Within six weeks of Uncle Dick Wootton's betrayal of the citadel to the frock coats of far-off State Street in Boston, where the Santa Fe did its banking, the carrier announced its intention of building up the Valley of the Arkansas from Pueblo through the almost impossibly narrow Royal Gorge to tap the now booming silver bonanzas of Leadville. Probably, since the Santa Fe had never for a minute taken its eye off the main chance, it contemplated a transcontinental connection with California over this central route but it announced its objective as Leadville. This alone was enough to raise General Palmer's blood pressure to Union League proportions. The Rio Grande regarded Leadville as already prospected and monumented for its own use.

In 1878, Leadville, precariously perched on top of Carbonate Hill, recapitulated with various improvements all the gold-rush excitements of the Old West that had gone before it: the Mother Lode, the Comstock, Fraser River, the Reese, the Coeur d'Alene. The year marked the fantastic discoveries of even greater bonanzas on Fryer Hill: the Little Chief, the Little Pittsburgh, New Discovery and Crysolite. Inflation sent prices of everything soaring. A mere shop in Chestnut Street or Harrison Avenue rented for $500 a month. "Rents are higher than in New York City", wrote an observer. Lots suitable for the building of mansions for the Carbonate Kings that had sold for $10 the year before now bore price tags of $10,000. Substantial brick buildings began to appear in the business districts, although the vast area covered with miners' shacks never divorced itself from a drabness that rivalled that of Liverpool or the mining slums of Wales.

Leadville now possessed two fine luxury hotels, the Grand and Clarendon, at the latter of which Lieutenant Governor of Colorado Horace A. W. Tabor rioted amidst blowsy mistresses and double magnums of champagne while wearing in his shirt front a diamond said to have belonged to Queen Isabella of Spain. In the Tabor Grand Opera House, the other Carbonate Kings joined Tabor in curtained boxes while they popped wine corks at third-rate soubrettes in tinsel costumes on its raked stage. Its architecture was described by Eugene Field as "modified Egyptian Moresque". There were 120 gorgeous bars in Leadville, one of which, the Great Saloon, made its owner $45,000 a year, while such dance halls as the Silver Thread, the Red Light, Tudor and Odeon were almost nightly the scenes of shootings and stabbings of primitive violence. Gambling was universal and wide open but of doubtful honesty.

To finance all these wealthy tumults, the established and proven deep diggings of Leadville, the Matchless, the Little Pittsburgh, the Crysolite, Vulture, Maid of Erin, Robert E. Lee and Carbonate were all in full production, creating tangible wealth at the rate of millions a month. The carbonate ores, when processed by the smelters, were poured into forty-pound pigs of combined lead and silver and sent off to New Jersey for refining. Leadville was producing more than 300 tons of pure silver a year.

Lawless, remote, primitive and incredibly rich, Leadville pirouetted in dizziest dithyrambs of illimitable bonanza. It was a plum ripe for the picking by any railroad with an eye to the main chance.

The contest between the Rio Grande and the Santa Fe for possession of the Royal Gorge was even more spectacular than the battle for the Raton. It made national headlines, saw the recruitment of entire armies of partisan pluguglies by the contestants, witnessed pitched battles between gunfighters and peace officers and raged through the courts of Colorado in a blizzard of legal writs, processes, opinions, judgments, injunctions, court orders, subpoenas, briefs and decisions. Most of the time the dust was so thick it was impossible to tell who was on top. Its elaborate and alternate advances and retreats, evasions, encirclements and contradances, all performed in an amazing saraband of bad feeling within the narrow confines of the Canyon of the Arkansas River even at this late date preclude any clear or coherent picture of just what happened to whom and when.

Its participants were by now veterans and bore the scars of other campaigns. Both De Remer and Morley, as the commanding generals, held a high opinion of each other as engineers and as free-for-all fighters with no holds barred. Morley, as a matter of record, had been in the employ of General Palmer a few years earlier and in 1871 had staked a line for the Rio Grande from Canon City to a point three miles above the Gorge itself, but no plat of construction had been filed in Denver and the Gorge was available to anyone who could seize and hold it. As far as Canon City there was room for a line of rails on either bank, but through the Gorge a narrow shelf provided foothold for a single right of way.

Grading crews and working parties from both railroads met head on in the abyss. Rock forts were built at strategic positions. Rock slides from the heights above buried tools and grading equipment, sometimes wiping out the right of way entirely. Blasts of giant powder rolled completed sections of track into the river. Survey stakes were relocated to the confusion of work parties. Sharpshooters harassed chainmen and other members of surveying teams. Storehouses caught fire and burned in the night. As in the struggle for the Raton, both parties tapped the wires of the opposition and soon latched onto the fine military technique of issuing bogus orders and sending falsified messages to confuse the enemy.

The Santa Fe, never unaware of the uses of publicity and propaganda, was agreeable to putting the war on a regional footing with itself in the role of the champion of progress and Kansas and the Rio Grande cast as the proponent of reactionary Colorado. To this end, it recruited an army of one hundred bad men, who arrived aboard a special armored train under the leadership of Bat Masterson, a celebrated peace officer from Dodge City, where he and Wyatt Earp had put the fear of God into tough-acting Texas trail hands in the days of the great cattle drives to the advancing railhead. Masterson's lieutenants in the Army of Kansas were such patriots as Ben Thompson of Texas and Doc Holliday, a Georgian who was real handy with shotguns, Bowie knives and whisky bottles and a good man to have around in uncertain times. Masterson even attempted to recruit Eddie Foy, the music hall comedian who had just had a successful season singing "Kalamazoo in Michigan" in Dodge. Foy declined.

Masterson's Army of Kansas, which arrived in Pueblo looking mean and swearing the way Uncle Toby asserted the armies used to swear in Flanders, promptly began coming apart at the seams. Despite the moral prejudices of General Palmer, the railroad town boasted the largest and most bedizened gaming houses anywhere in the West. The hired hard cases got snared in its "six faro banks, four roulette wheels, one Hieronymous bowl, four tables for hazard and craps, two for stud poker, one for short faro, one for vingt-et-un and one for high suit". There were also back rooms for daily drawings of policy and keno, a monster free lunch, and, of course, drinks in a variety and plenitude to satisfy even railroaders in an age that knew no rule G. The management of the Rio Grande shrewdly assured the management of this pavillion of pleasures of complete immunity from molestation by the law so long as the Santa Fe gangsters were kept occupied.

The battle front in and around the Valley of the Arkansas was largely characterized by mock heroic stances, barroom ruffling and rodomontade on the part of all concerned. Partisans met with Dion Boucicault breathings of defiance and, after smashing up the back bar and hurling a few empties at each other's heads, retired in perfect amity to another oasis down the street. "Most of it was noise," says David Lavender, official historian of Colorado's most opulent folklore. "There was a deal of shooting and fisticuffing . . . Several heads were broken and perhaps a man or two killed . . . Certainly matters would have been worse had not Bat Masterson sold out in a secret deal with officials of the Rio Grande."

In the end, through a series of reversed court decisions that would have proved light reading for Burke or Chief Justice Holmes, the Rio Grande came out top dog. Unnoticed in the alarms and excursions among the switch stands, Jay Gould had bought control of the Rio Grande. Here was an opponent far more formidable to the Santa Fe than General Palmer's gaggle of Denver bankers and rented judges. Gould was in a position to raise several kinds of assorted hell with the Santa Fe's Eastern financing and was not the sort of enemy to be encouraged when New York moneybags foregathered amidst thickets of potted palms in Delmonico's or the Waldorf's Amen Corner.

The Santa Fe accepted $1,400,000 cash on the barrel head for the track it had already laid in the Royal Gorge and crossed its corporate heart not to attempt any further invasion of Leadville. In return, the Rio Grande agreed to forswear the Santa Fe Trail as a route to the Southwest, a promise which it compromised on a small scale in the nineties, when it took over a connection with the old New Mexican pueblo at Santa Fe known as the Texas, Santa Fe & Northern Railway and operated it for four decades as the celebrated "Chili Line" from Santa Fe to Antonito.

General Palmer's ambition for a continental railroad proved him by no means lacking in foresight and, as a detail of his plan to achieve a Utah terminal for his narrow gauge operations, he acquired at the Salt Lake end of his prospective mainline a property known as The Rio Grande Western. This was eventually to be combined with the D&RG as the Denver & Rio Grande Western of its ultimate and still existing corporate title. Construction of the Rio Grande Western was begun in 1881 and the first fifty miles from Salt Lake to Springville were completed in the same year. From there to Detour, a span of thirty miles, there was a nowhere-to-nowhere narrow gauge already in faltering operation and known as the Utah & Pleasant Valley Railroad which the General purchased outright. Soldier Summit was reached by a four per cent grade up a long, steep ravine in the escarpment of the Wasatch Plateau and was crossed early in 1882, the year in which the Denver & Rio Grande building westward from Gunnison achieved Grand Junction via the Black Canyon of the Gunnison River. In April, 1883, the track gangs crossed into Colorado and on May 21, a sort of narrow gauge promontory was celebrated when they joined the oncoming iron of the Denver & Rio Grande at Desert, Utah. An extension was opened from Salt Lake to Ogden and General Palmer had achieved a through narrow gauge mainline 771 miles long from Denver to Ogden, where it connected with the standard gauge Overland mainline of the Central Pacific for through traffic to California.

Luxuriously upholstered varnish trains made the run "through the Rockies, not around them" from Denver to the capital of the Saints in forty-one hours with mail and express cars carrying head-end revenue, coaches, standard Pullmans, tourist sleepers and diminutive diners as their daily consist. The little, lightweight engines of the period, *Ptarmigan, Eagle River, Ten Mile* and *Fort De Remer* (the last named for the line's first chief engineer at the time of the Santa Fe wars), because of their delicate and jewellike side motion and valve gear were locally known as "sewing machines" and seldom had occasion to exceed speeds of forty miles an hour, even on the most inviting tangents.

Travelers on the through trains, Eastern capitalists in broadcloth tail coats, English milords in ratcatcher suits and high gaiters, young men fresh out of Harvard and eager to follow the dictum of Horace Greeley, all lived high on the hog aboard the Rio Grande's diners. The menus that have come down to us invest the lightest collation with Lucullan overtones. Hock and champagne were the acceptable wines for breakfast; quail, partridge, venison and antelope abounded among the entrees. Colorado steer meat began to emerge on the national consciousness in the form of *filets* for two bits and porterhouse for seventy-five cents, and the Rocky Mountain trout from the state's first commercial hatcheries was becoming a Rio Grande staple, as it has been ever since.

From Denver City by Cherry Creek to the far side of the Wasatch in the Utah meadows and from the Black Canyon of the Gunnison as far south as ancestral Taos and the Plaza at Santa Fe, the smoke of the Rio Grande's teapot locomotives ascended to heaven and the red markers of its going diminished in the high passes at night. Throughout the Shining Mountains the exhaust of reciprocating steam locomotives was becoming the pulse of life in a new economy.

The microcosmic satisfactions of the narrow gauge transcontinental lasted less than a decade and late in the eighties it became apparent that both the density of traffic and the necessity of interchange of freight cars with standard connecting railroads made widening the track an imperative. Standard gauge rails supplemented the three-foot iron all along the Royal Gorge route, and a third rail was retained for the accommodation of narrow gauge equipment as far south as Pueblo and up the valley of the Arkansas to Leadville until well into the twentieth century. The high water mark of the three-foot track was achieved in 1889, when the recession from narrow gauge that has continued to this day set in. Branch lines and stub tracks connecting with the remaining three-foot business tracks continued to be graded, but in ever decreasing mileage.

The reasons for broad gauging the Rio Grande's mainlines were not altogether internal or operational in their origin, but resulted from outside pressures in the form of threatened competition. In November of 1883, a group of Colorado financiers and industrialists met right in General Palmer's own home town and favorite real estate project of Colorado Springs to organize the Colorado Midland Railroad which was to build a standard gauge competitive carrier directly from the Springs to Salt Lake City. The Midland got under way briskly and, in a very short time, broad gauge tracks were being laid to salient points in what had been to date the Rio Grande's own private preserve: Buena Vista, then Leadville, and on to Aspen, Glenwood Springs and New Castle.

A good deal of Colorado's sentiment went into the construction of the Midland, which somehow secured a hold on local affections never achieved by the

HOWARD FOGG

The narrow gauge through train of the Denver & Rio Grande between Denver and its Utah connections at Salt Lake and Ogden ascended Marshall Pass, paused briefly to refresh its operating economy, pick up passengers and set out the mail at Gunnison and then headed for Montrose through the gloomy and cavernous Black Canyon of the Gunnison River. Its diminutive yet handsomely appointed cars included head-end revenue, coaches, a diner whose opulent menu was celebrated among voyagers everywhere, a through Pullman sleeper, and as like as not, a business car of one of the road's ranking executives, possibly even General William J. Palmer himself. It double headed through the Black Canyon and the artist has shown it with No. 222, a workhorse locomotive built by Grant in 1882 as helper, and No. 176, a Baldwin product as road engine. Black indeed flows Gunnison Water below the roadbed, but Colorado skies were blue above, for it was the year 1885 and all the world was young.

cold-blooded operations of General Palmer and the lofty moral tone with which he contrived to invest projects that were conspicuously ruthless. The Midland was a railroad of style and elegance to match the narrow gauge and much of its right of way up Ute Pass and across South Park was comparable to the well-advertised "Scenic Route of the World". The Midland and the Rio Grande got together on a basis of economy to operate a single track for both roads between Grand Junction and New Castle, but no love was lost between them and the Rio Grande went ahead with its program of standardization with what celerity its finances allowed.

Even after the diversion of through transcontinental traffic to the standard gauge over Tennessee Pass, the Gunnison-Montrose route prospered as a narrow gauge carrier of both passengers and freight in ponderable quantities.

Many distinguished names in the tally of the nation's great rode the narrow gauges in their happy heyday and remembered homely adventures and hairbreadth 'scapes by tunnel and trestle for years afterward. None recalls more vividly than Bruce Catton, most distinguished of all chroniclers of the Civil War and today editor of *American Heritage*.

"Here," he wrote the authors of this volume, "is a brief fill-in of my 'Perils-of-Pauline' experience on the Colorado narrow gauge:

It happened back in (I think) 1932, thereabouts, anyway. My wife and I were visiting my brother, who then lived in Montrose, over 'way beyond the continental divide, and one day, for no very good reason, a number of us drove to a way station named Sapinero; this was on the narrow gauge line of the Denver & Rio Grande Western which ran from Salida to Montrose, where I think it met a standard gauge line that ran down to Grand Junction. Anyway, at Sapinero we got out of the car and hiked up some canyon or other, following the narrow gauge line; the railroad presently crossed the canyon on a trestle and we had no better sense than to cross on that trestle. (Sure, I'd been taught never to walk on a railroad bridge, but we did it anyhow.)

After inspecting the far side of the canyon, we began to return. The party got strung out and my wife and I, with my brother's seven-year-old son, were out in the exact middle of the thing; everybody else had finished the crossing. All of a sudden around the corner in the canyon, there was a shrill whistle and along came the afternoon passenger train for Salida heading straight toward us and coming, as it seemed then, with uncommon speed and ferocity. Not having been built for pedestrian traffic, this trestle was nothing but ties and rails and the nearest solid ground was about one hundred feet away, straight down—a collection of very nasty looking rocks, quite jagged.

Fortunately, the thirty feet or so of the mid-section of this trestle had overlength ties; they stuck out about eighteen inches farther than the ordinary tie does and a four by four stringer lay on top of them parallel with the rail, running about where the end of the tie normally comes. (I hope this is clear, though I doubt it.) Somehow we managed to lie down on the tie ends outside of the stringer, hugging same with our left arms, with our right arms and legs sort of floating off in space. I remember pushing the rump of my small nephew down flat, trying to deflate my own stomach, and hoping that my wife (who was out of sight behind me) was going to make out all right; and as this snorting monster of a train approached, I kept watching the overhanging steps trying to figure if they would clear us. Somehow that train looked as big and as ominous as the *Broadway Limited.* Not to keep you in suspense, we had plenty of clearance and were not knocked off into the gulch; the train passed, we rolled to the left, got to our feet, and tottered feebly to the end of the trestle and safety.

That's all there is to the story and, as you can see, it is really not much of a yarn. I suppose, looking back, if we had just stood still and waved our arms the thing would have come to a halt in time; it couldn't really have been going very fast and those little narrow gauge trains must have been able to stop on a dime. We probably would have had some interesting comments from the train crew, though.

We had been collecting pretty colored rocks with some vague idea of using them in a rock garden back home and had our arms full when that damn train suddenly appeared. None of us can remember doing anything about those stones; all anybody knows is that after the train had passed, the stones were not around anywhere. I still do not have a rock garden.

That narrow gauge was quite an outfit. A week or so later we took it back to Salida, where we transferred to the main stem. I remember the parlor car was a doll's house sort of business; nice little wicker chairs, with just enough room between them for the conductor and porter to walk back and forth. I believe that particular line has been abandoned by now. Too bad; it was very picturesque and it sure gave me the scare of my life, once."

Aside from its mainline traffickings across Colorado to Utah and Salt Lake and its next most populous business track to Alamosa and Durango, the Rio Grande began a series of skirmishes with the Rocky Mountain geography that found it proprietor of a score of short lines, spurs and branches hardly any of which could or would ever have been surveyed for standard operations.

Once firmly established at Durango, it headed a year later up the Canyon of Animas to the booming town of Silverton, obviously named for the mining that dominated its existence, forty-five miles to the north through some of the most spectacular scenery in the North American continent. Through sleepers from Denver were soon thereafter scheduled to this inaccessible *cul-de-sac* in the San Juan mountains.

From the Durango-Alamosa track a stub was built to Pagosa Springs, a health spa with curative waters. A branch went from Alamosa to Wagon Wheel Gap and thence to Creede, a rough-and-ready mining town of brief duration whose boom collapsed in 1893 when the Sherman Act shattered the entire economy of precious metals of the mountain area. It was of Creede that Cy Warman, the railroad poet, penned his immortal couplet:

"It's day all day in daytime
And there is no night in Creede."

Lake City became terminal of a branch line, and from Poncha Junction a spur famous for its switchbacks led up to the mines at Monarch. There was, of course, the famed Chili route from Antonito to Santa Fe, and from Salida to Alamosa a fifty-three mile tangent ran down through the San Luis valley between the continental divide and the Sangre de Cristo mountains. From Montrose on the Gunnison mainline, there was a stub leading to a connection with Otto Mears's Rio Grande Southern at Ridgway and on to the mountain fastness in Box Canyon occupied by Ouray.

Later the Crested Butte branch was extended to Floresta and an interesting branch was the Grape Creek line to Silver Cliff. Still another, and of exceptional

AUTHOR'S COLLECTION

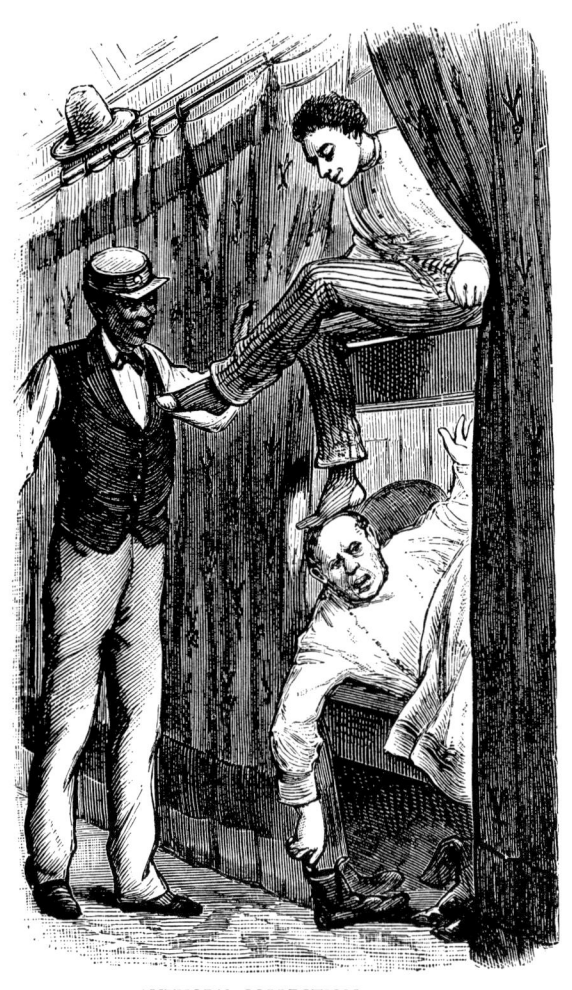

The most celebrated of all the many photographs taken along the narrow gauges of Colorado in their heyday and prime was William H. Jackson's wet plate of the Silverton Train posed above the Canyon of Animas at Rockwood headed south on the run to Durango. Because in the eighties halftones for the reproduction of photographs were nowhere near as satisfactory as stone engravings, the editors of *Harper's Weekly*, who wished to run the picture covering the center spread of their magazine, had a staff artist translate the Jackson photograph into the line drawing of gloomy grandeur reproduced on the page opposite. The fascinations of travel aboard the three-foot cars never failed to interest the reading public of the period and on this page are two sketches by members of the Frank Leslie Expedition to report on the West in the late seventies. The one at the left was captioned "Must Step Somewhere" and belongs to the almost limitless category of anecdota and folklore evoked by the open berth Pullman sleeping car. Below is a narrow gauge washroom aboard a Rocky Mountain sleeping train of the same period, obviously without the innovation of running hot water under pressure which was evolved with such resounding repurcussions as one of the innovations aboard General Palmer's narrow gauge "house car," *Nomad*.

AUTHOR'S COLLECTION

concern to connoissuers of such matters, was the Calumet branch which started at Brown Canyon north of Salida and climbed to Calumet, a distance of about seven miles with grades that ranged up to an incredible 7.7 per cent.

Early in the eighties, the rival Denver, South Park & Pacific built a three-foot gauge connection from Gunnison, whose traffic it was by now sharing with the Rio Grande, to Castleton and Baldwin, and when in 1910 the Alpine Tunnel was closed leaving the Quartz-Gunnison-Baldwin segment without connection with the rest of the Colorado & Southern, an arrangement was made with the D&RG to operate the line. In 1937, the Baldwin branch became the property of the D&RGW by gift of the C&S.

Toward the end of the Rio Grande's era of expansion, when it was already beginning to retreat from worked-out mining camps and abandoned diggings, it indulged in one of the few fanciful and eccentric gestures in its long career in the form of a standard gauge branch reaching from Durango across the New Mexican line to Farmington. The Farmington branch turned out to be a true sport in the biological sense of the word and had the distinction, some twenty years later, of being rebuilt to narrow gauge, perhaps the only railroad in the American record in this manner to defy a tide universally turning in the opposite direction.

On none of the Rio Grande's narrow gauge runs was romance more conspicuously part of the conductor's wheel report than the still-operating forty-five mile Silverton branch. So strong a hold did the route above the yawning Canyon of Animas River (named the Rio de los Animas Perdidas a full century earlier by good Father Escalante), have on the popular imagination of nearly three full generations of Western and railroad-minded Americans that passenger service over its forty-five miles of breath-taking right of way survived when all other narrow gauge passenger routes were abandoned. As this is being written in the year 1958, the Silverton Train is the only regularly scheduled narrow gauge passenger operation anywhere in the United States and, as a tourist attraction, it is a predominant factor in the vital economy of both Durango and Silverton.

In the early years of Silverton's emergence as the seat of San Juan County it boasted a free-wheeling population of 4,000 prospectors, hard-rock miners, speculators, promoters, saloon keepers, prostitutes and monte throwers. In flourishing operation were all the accustomed honky-tonks and fandango houses and thirty gorgeous saloons catered to the inextinguishable thirst of miners who, on Saturday night, converged on Silverton as the regional cosmopolis from Howardsville, Animas Forks, Middletown and Mineral Point. The Rio Grande arrived in 1882, nicely timed to coincide with the camp's banner year of production when its mines yielded nearly $20,000,000 in gold and silver ore. So wild and lawless was Silverton's night life and so frequent its murders and incidental shootings at this time that Bat Masterson was imported from Dodge City and for a short period the community knew a reign of vigilante law that effectively put an end to assassination, at least as a casual recreation.

The first passenger train came into town over the Fourth of July, 1882, and patriotism and civic pride dictated a communal drunk still remembered throughout the San Juan as the most sensational whisky doin's in the record.

Ore shipments were immediate and heavy from the mines dominated by Silverton's 13,500 foot peaks: the Shenandoah Dives, Royal Tiger, Buffalo Boy, Black Prince, Highland Mary, Coming Wonder, Gold King, Sunnyside, Treasure Mountain and Polar Star. Largely, the ores were reduced at Durango but some of the recoveries were impervious to local treatment and went over the rails to the great outer world, some as far as Wales.

Passenger service, too, was brisk and profitable and a celebrated and much-copied photograph by Jackson in the nineties shows the Silverton Train posed on the rocky shelf at Rockwood double-headed with seven coaches. Overnight sleepers made the run of nearly 500 miles to Denver and the private cars of nabobs and business cars of the management were a commonplace on the private car siding at Silverton.

The town's night life continued to be boisterous, but less lethal as overtones of civilization rode in on the steamcars. One evening a drummer was sitting minding his manners in the Hub Saloon when the wife of a colored Pullman porter on the night run upset the reigning decorum as she flounced through in search of her errant spouse. "If I don't find that coon, there's going to be a hot time in the old town tonight," she muttered, and the drummer fetched by the homely phrase, went on to write a song called "There'll be a Hot Time in the Old Town Tonight".

On another occasion, at the height of Silverton's evil eminence as a wide open town, a passenger who rode in on the narrow gauge was the former Dodge City celebrity, Bat Masterson, now City Marshal of Trinidad, in search of his old comrade-at-arms, Wyatt Earp. Masterson brought tidings that their old friend, Luke Short, the deadly gambler and one of the most fearless gunmen, was having a rough time back in Dodge in their absence, having been put upon shamefully by Mayor A. B. Webster, who ran rival gaming rooms and was trying to move Short out of town. Never one to desert a friend and inflamed by the unethical aspects of the deal, Earp took leave of Silverton and headed east on the cars with Masterson, only pausing at Durango to send significant telegrams to various parts of the West. The wires were to four of the most skilled and coolest gunslingers of the age, Jack Vermillion, Johnny Green, Johnny Millsap and Dan Tipton, who shortly converged on Dodge City together with Earp and Masterson. On the outskirts of town they picked up Prairie Dog Dave Morrow and, as a delegation embracing enough wholesale massacre to depopulate half of Kansas, they called in a body on Mayor Webster. The Mayor saw the error of his ways and agreed that he had perhaps acted hastily in riding herd on good old Luke Short. The men who tamed Dodge City at Earp's rallying cry constituted perhaps the greatest single group of gunfighters ever assembled under a united banner in the history of the Old West.

Silverton continued to boom well into the twentieth century. Otto Mears's three short line narrow gauges probing the mountains behind Silverton added to the ore carloadings that continued in ever diminishing quantities until 1952, when the last consignment was sent from the Shenandoah-Dives. Winter often saw Silverton cut off from the outer world, sometimes for protracted periods when snowslides of mountainous proportions defied efforts of the railroad to penetrate them. In 1906, snow fell for eight days continuously and twenty men were lost in the succession of slides which wrecked whole mining camps and entombed outlying shacks whose residents were not discovered until spring.

Traffic on the Silverton branch followed the graph of mining, always downward until, during the 1941 war, a mixed train twice a week with passengers riding the caboose and a single combine was sufficient for the requirements of the Community.

Silverton's rediscovery by an avalanche of tourists was part of the great wave of postwar travel within the United States and the far-reaching revival of the popularity of the Old West. It was no secret that Al Perlman, general manager at the time of the Rio Grande and known throughout Colorado as "the butcher boy" for his ruthless elimination of unprofitable operations, had in mind the complete abandonment of all narrow gauge operations of any sort. In his regime, the daily *San Juan* between Durango and Alamosa was suspended and the way paved for the abandonment of the original transcontinental mainline between Salida and Montrose via Gunnison. Perlman had no animus against the narrow gauge, but neither had he any lingering sentiment and he eventually went on to even more spectacular economies as president of the New York Central.

Only the Silverton Train remained and its life was in constant jeopardy as accountants ran wild and unhindered in the railroad's main offices at Denver. But what had once been a mere trickle of tourists suddenly became a torrent. Space on what coaches and combines the road could muster for the Silverton run was sold out weeks in advance and motorists whose sole objective was Durango and a ride to yesterday aboard the steamcars clogged the breathless highway at Wolf Creek Pass for weeks on end in summer months.

The Silverton operation was found to be turning a substantial if not gaudy profit. The Rio Grande, which understood the language of money while stone deaf in matters of sentiment, gathered a pool of lemon-yellow coaches and combines and assigned special train crews versed in regional lore and legend to the run. The train reverted to a daily in summer months, invariably crowded to its capacity of 300 cash customers paying $4.45 each for the ninety mile round trip.

The fame of the Silverton Train gave vitality to the entire economy of the countryside. At Silverton the venerable Imperial Hotel was completely reactivated in Victorian style by an amiable Texas moneybags named Winfield Morten and re-named The Grand Imperial. Its restaurant blossomed with wall-to-wall carpets and the menu displayed unsuspected elegance, with broiled African lobster tails, New York cut steaks and London broil. A wine card, reminiscent of the wine list on Otto Mears's once proud narrow gauge diner, *Animas Forks,* bristled with such arrangements as Texas Fizz (for Mr. Morten), Pink Lady, Cuba Libra, Grasshopper, Stinger, Salty Dog, Screwdriver and Vodka Collins—devisings that would have bugged the eyes of the sourdoughs whose repertory of potables began and ended with Bourbon and branch.

At Durango, the impact of the Silverton Train on the local economy was even more dramatic. The Strater Hotel that had dozed through the decades as a favored resort of whisky drummers, farm implement salesmen, and a sprinkling of wildflower fanciers and amateur photographers representing pure tourism, suddenly found its rooms and restaurant in urgent requisition and a beautiful river of currency flowing in the direction of its cash till. Rooms in the back of the house overlooking the D&RGW freight yard that had formerly been the last to rent attracted special demand when the management advertised: "Hear the Trains Whistle at Night." The Strater bar, formerly a prudent premises in the cellarage, was brought bodily streetside and decorated as the Diamond Belle Saloon. Barroom nudes in bank vault frames of purest gold adorned the brocaded walls. A professor in derby and sleeve suspenders pounded out barbershop tunes and waitresses in scanty attire distributed sidecars and Ramos fizzes among the customers. The Strater newsstand did a land-office business in engineer's caps, fireman's scarves, jumbo post cards of the narrow gauge engines and certificates attesting that the holder had ridden the Silverton Train for a fact.

Elsewhere in downtown Durango, restaurants within whistle screech of the depot advertised special "Railroad Breakfasts" and box lunches to take aboard the train. Banker Camp, the grand old man of the San Juan, took to walking down to the depot of an afternoon to watch the train come in, much as he had done in his youth a full half century before. A ponderable part of Durango's life was once more synchronized with the panting exhaust of narrow gauge engines working steam as they headed out of town.

Down the years the Denver & Rio Grande Railroad and its eventual consolidation as the D&RGW has been with the exception of mining itself, the most important single fact in the economy and life of Colorado. It came into being as the state was emerging upon the consciousness of the nation and was itself a pioneer agency of exploration and high adventure, one with the Pikes-Peak-or-Bust prospector, the Mountain Men, the Long Hunters, and the great tradition of coaching and express transport whose thorough-braced Concord coaches themselves at last gave place to the now almost legendary cars and engines of the narrow gauge.

In no state of the Union did railroad transport occupy so exalted a position, not only in the general economy of the community but in the awareness and imagination of men, as in Colorado and the density of steam carriers at the zenith of their fortunes was so great that the 1908 edition of Rand & McNally's *Enlarged Business Atlas* showed no fewer than thirty different roads in operation and five express companies.

Of all the railroads that have come and gone in Colorado, the Rio Grande with its modest beginnings in three-foot gauge has been the most tenacious and abiding. The mutations of corporate reformation and reactivation have left its imprint upon the face of the land unchanged. Now, in an age of abandonments, consolidations and a new profile of operations, it is hard to discern vestigial traces of its original simplicities of country landfaring. But the Rio Grande was the first of the narrow gauges in the region; it was the pioneer, and this panache of splendor must cleave to its memory forever.

EDGAR T. MEADE, JR.

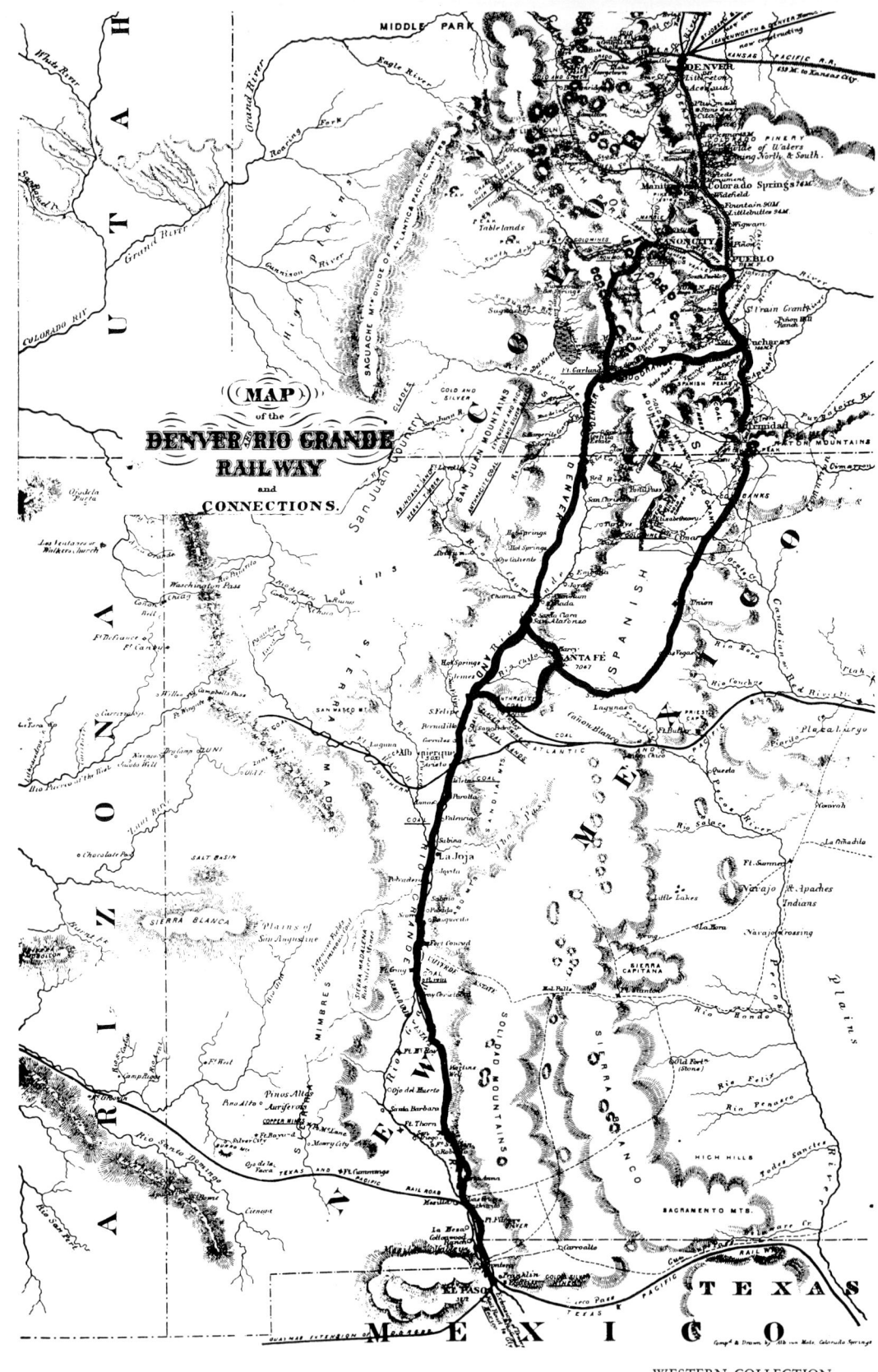

WESTERN COLLECTION

Illustrating one of the most optimistic railroad projects in the record, the map shown here was presented by General Palmer at the directors' meeting of the Denver & Rio Grande Railroad on the perhaps significant date April 1, 1873. It shows two branches of the narrow gauge, one via the Raton Pass and the other by way of the Fort Garland Extension converging on Santa Fe and following the Rio Grande itself straight to Old Mexico. A few years later found the General's tracklayers laying the light iron through Chama for Durango, in the Black Canyon of the Gunnison, up Animas to Silverton and indeed almost anywhere except to the El Paso so hopefully designated on this map.

Anger and frustration were not the only elements to enter into the early years of the Rio Grande. There was fun, too, as is attested by this photograph of an excursion group beside the rails at the summit of Veta Pass. Among them was an early mayor of Denver named Wolf Londoner, who was noted as a powerful man with the bottle, and the caption to the picture read: "Veta Pass - 9,339 Feet Above Sea Level, But Not More Elevated Than Wolf Londoner's Tea Party. Mr. Londoner, with the smile that is so sweetly becoming to him, represented that the party was athirst." And it may be presumed that steps were taken to remedy this condition among the whiskers and frock coats of this atmospheric group. BELOW: A Jackson photograph showing a work train at Toltec Tunnel shortly after its completion.

TWO PHOTOS: WESTERN COLLECTION

Legend clustered thickly around the patrician person of General William Jackson Palmer, founder of the fortunes of the Rio Grande railroad and no man to shirk a fight. He was outraged when *The Rocky Mountain News* printed the intelligence that aboard his business car *Nomad* the master bedroom, with its brass bed as depicted on the page opposite, boasted both hot and cold running water. As an aristocrat, he resented the invasion of his privacy; as an old campaigner, he resented the implication of a luxurious way of life and immediately ordered the hot water disconnected. Probably the hot water was replaced once the general had time to recover from his pique, for he wrote to the future Mrs. Palmer: "I am having a nice house car made just convenient for you and me to travel up and down when business demands and this car will have every convenience of living while in motion." In its active lifetime *Nomad* knew many notables, such as Cecil Rhodes, Otto Mears, Theodore Roosevelt. Aboard it President U. S. Grant rode the first Rio Grande train into Leadville. It was, too, a sensation in a railroad-minded generation and was exhibited at the St. Louis World's Fair in 1904, the San Francisco Fair of 1915 and at Chicago's Century of Progress in 1933. Today a restoration of *Nomad* is on the private car track of the D&RGW at Durango, the property of H. B. Wood and Ted M. White, a well-to-do oil man with large holdings in the San Juan, and it is without any doubt at all the only narrow gauge car in operable commission to be privately owned in the United States.

LUCIUS BEEBE

WESTERN COLLECTION

THREE PHOTOS: DURANGO HERALD-NEWS

The Denver & Rio Grande's narrow gauge line over Veta Pass, originally known as the Fort Garland Extension, at the time of its construction was the highest railroad pass in the world (9,220 feet) and excited widespread interest, as is suggested by the montage of drawings made by a staff artist for Frank Leslie's *Illustrated Weekly Newspaper* in 1881. Somewhat arbitrary artistically but of interest to the railroad historian is the view of Antonito, showing the westbound track heading for Durango and the southbound rails pointing toward Santa Fe via the Chili Line, in the same relationship in which they remained until the abandonment of the Santa Fe branch in 1940. On this page the Rio Grande's No. 26 is pictured on the stub line at Manitou for a radiant profile of Colorado railroading in the year 1872. The long-bearded train captain, silk-hatted driver of the depot hack, beer barrels from the Denver Brewery and notice of villa lots for sale by the railroad company as part of General Palmer's program of real estate promotion along its right of way, all are the fragrant properties of far away and long ago in the shadow of Pike's Peak.

THE MILL.

WESTERN COLLECTION

TWO PICTURES: WESTERN COLLECTION

When the route up the Valley of the Arkansas where once Bent's Fort had dominated the Rocky Mountain fur trade was completed by the Rio Grande, it was laid, conforming to all other trackage of the road, to three-foot gauge as shown in the top photograph of the famed Hanging Bridge. Although a third rail was laid as part of the standardization of the transcontinental route over Tennessee Pass in 1891, the narrow gauge remained available to traffic and stayed spiked into Leadville until 1925. When Theodore Roosevelt toured the West in 1903 and caused his special train to pause at the Hanging Bridge, the two gauge track was very much in evidence in the official photograph of the moment. Switchers and road engines alike were fitted with multiple couplings or drawbars adaptable to either type of rolling stock and long after the mainline carried only standard gauge passenger trains, merchandise rolled on the three-foot tracks as an important part in the overall economy of the carrier.

TWO PHOTOS: WESTERN COLLECTION

The war between the Rio Grande and the Santa Fe for the right of way up the Royal Gorge of the Arkansas, on the page opposite, was characterized by a great deal of threatening language and show of force, but actual combat was largely confined to courtrooms and judge's chambers in Denver. The eventual victory of the Rio Grande compensated, in part at least, for the loss in earlier contest of the pass over the Raton. In the upper photograph on the page opposite General Palmer's embattled partisans rally at Fort De Remer, named for the Rio Grande's chief engineer, to resist to the death the bottle scarred veterans of Bat Masterson's "Army of Kansas."
BELOW: a reception committee of Colorado loyalists waits on the arrival of a trainload of Santa Fe hirelings at Pueblo.

LUCIUS BEEBE

WESTERN COLLECTION: WILLIAM H. JACKSON

On the page opposite is a tranquil stretch of Animas in Durango Meadows, as seen from the rear platform of a business car attached to the Silverton train, while (BELOW), in a classic wet plate by Jackson, a Rio Grande "Jackson Special" pauses in the seventies beside the banks of the Grand River. On this page a Rio Grande Southern merchandise, with No. 42 on the business end and a helper behind, follows the course of the San Miguel near Placerville. On the same page the South Park's tank at Dillon on the Keystone Branch reminds of the ever-present need for fuel water in abundance in the age of steam.

OTTO PERRY

Wherever it was practicable, the wild, foaming rivers of Colorado and, say their names with bugles, Clear Creek, the River of Lost Souls, Gunnison, the Blue, San Miguel and the Rio Grande of corporate titles and spacious legend, showed the way for the railroad builders to follow. The South Platte was the monumented claim of the South Park; the first transcontinental narrow gauge main line of General Palmer followed the Arkansas past the site of Bent's Fort and again threaded the Black Canyon of the Gunnison; Otto Mears's toll road from Ridgway to Telluride had marched beside the San Miguel and so did the tracks of the Rio Grande Southern. Above the Canyon of Animas the Silverton branch of the D&RG headed toward Red Mountain and the well-remembered Mears short lines out of Silverton, each according to water level survey, followed Mineral Creek, Cement Creek and Animas to their several destinations. Ohio Creek, Slate River and Roaring Fork all showed the way the three-foot rails should go.

RICHARD B. JACKSON

FOUR PHOTOS: COURTESY PULLMAN STANDARD

In 1871, when the Denver & Rio Grande ordered the first narrow gauge passenger cars from the shops of Jackson & Sharp in Wilmington, Delaware, so great was the public interest in what promised to be an important new aspect of railroading that a sketch artist from the staff of *Frank Leslie's Weekly* was promptly dispatched to the West Philadelphia yards of the Pennsylvania Railroad, where the equipment was on view before going into service in Colorado. "The cars exhibit every convenience imaginable and leave few or no comforts to be desired," said *Leslie's* in its next issue, where it ran this drawing to show the interior and the manner of staggering single and double seats for equable distribution of weight. In the official builder's photograph (BELOW) note that the car *Denver*, in the absence of three-foot rails, was mounted for handling on a specially constructed length of narrow gauge track. On the page opposite are shown standard gauge baggage and passenger coaches as they were outshopped for the railroad a few years later by Pullman at his Detroit car shops.

WESTERN COLLECTION

DENVER & RIO GRANDE ARCHIVES

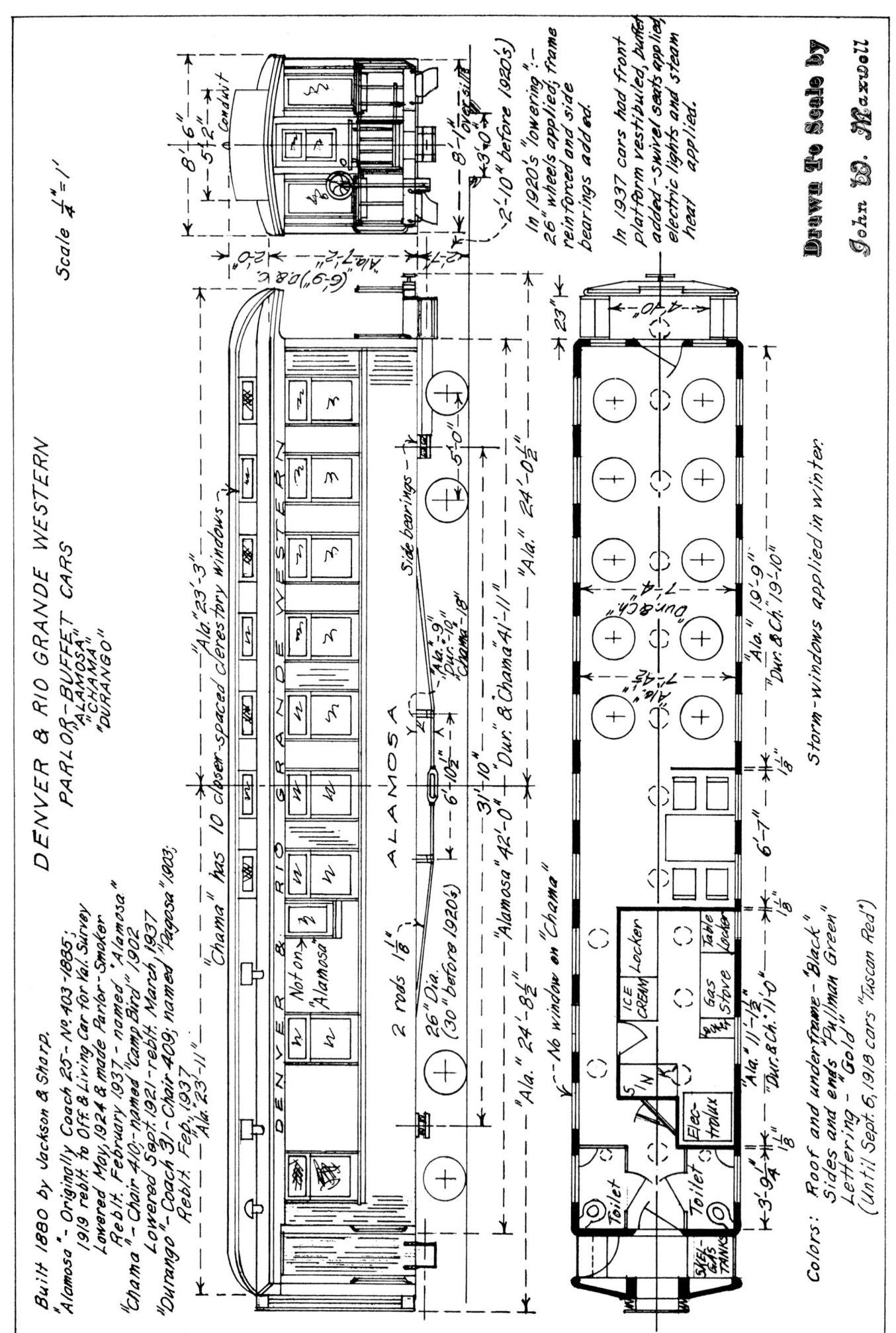

ARTHUR DUBIN COLLECTION

In its early days the D&RG was liberal in its orders for luxury rolling stock in the form of sleeping cars, parlor cars, diners, club and observation lounges and business cars for important executives. The sleeping car *Toltec* shown above, in conformance to narrow gauge practice and Palmer's law, had ten sections and berths were for single occupancy only. The car *Alamosa*, architect's drawings of which appear on the opposite page, lasted from 1880 in various redactions down to the end of passenger service between Alamosa and Durango in the consist of the daily *San Juan* (BELOW) and supplied de luxe transport for two whole generations of travelers in the narrow gauge country of Colorado.

RICHARD B. JACKSON

As long as the Rio Grande's transcontinental main line followed over Marshall Pass and the Black Canyon of the Gunnison, the symbol and insigne of the railroad was the Currecanti Needle, a rock pinnacle pointing skyward a few miles east of Cimmaron and photographed here by William H. Jackson. At the time the below photograph of the roundhouse at Salida was exposed by another Jackson about 1900, standard gauge track was beginning to crowd the three-foot rails, although the profile of yesterday was still visible in diamond stacks and oil-burning headlights. Both narrow and standard tracks ran together as far as Leadville until 1925 and the three-foot gauge only disappeared completely from the Salida yards in the fiftys, when the branch to Monarch was relaid to standard.

WESTERN COLLECTION: W. H. JACKSON

WESTERN COLLECTION: V. G. JACKSON

Narrow gauge passenger equipment in the early days of the Rio Grande and its Colorado neighbors inclined toward what was known as "elegance" in the *decor* of Pullmans and dining cars and more or less Spartan simplicity in ordinary day coaches, combines and smokers. Open platforms were the rule, coal or Pintsch patent gas lamps illuminated the interiors and swung menacingly as the cars progressed over the uneven right of way, and deceleration was accomplished at first by Ames vacuum brakes and later by Westinghouse. Although the illusion of splendor was maintained through the agency of red plush and plate glass, a traveler of 1958 accustomed to air conditioning and rubber draft gear would have found the cars less than luxurious. In the below photograph of Denver's Union Depot in the eighties, three rails to accomodate both gauges were laid on all tracks and honored names in the annals of the Old West identified the offices of Wells Fargo & Co., the Pacific Express Co. and the Denver & Rio Grande Rwy. Express. A Union Pacific standard gauge train, headed toward Cheyenne behind No. 415 is just about to highball.

ROBERT HALE

WESTERN COLLECTION: W. H. JACKSON

Wine List

		QTS.	PTS.
CHAMPAGNES	G. H. Mumm & Co., Extra Dry	4.00	2.00
	Pommery & Greno "Sec"	4.00	2.00
	Moet & Chandon White Seal	4.00	2.00
	Dry Monopole H. & Co., Extra	4.00	2.00
	Veuve Cliquot, Yellow Label	4.00	2.00
	Cook's Imperial	2.00	1.25
	Ruinart Vin Brut, half pts. only, 1.00		
WHITE WINES	Latour Blanche, Cruse Fils Freres	2.50	1.50
	Haut Sauterne, Cruse Fils Freres	2.00	1.00
CLARETS	St. Julien, Cruse Fils Freres	1.25	.75
	Pontet Canet, Cruse Fils Freres	2.00	1.00
	Chateau La Rose, Cruse Fils Freres	2.50	1.50
RHINE WINES	Rudesheimer, Carl Acker	2.00	1.00
	Niersteiner, Carl Acker	1.50	.75
CALIFORNIA WINES	Chablis (C. C. McIver)	.75	.50
	Linda Vista Zinfandel (C. C. McIver)	.75	.50
	Riesling Anslese (C. C. McIver)	.75	.50
	Sauterne (Cresta Blanca), (1-2 Pts., 25)	.75	.50
	St. Julien (Cresta Blanca)	.75	.50

ALES, BEERS, ETC.		
Bass & Co., D. H. & W. L.		.30
Guinness Extra Stout		.30
Zang's, Neff's and Coor's Denver Beers		.20
Salt Lake, Fisher, Wagner and Margett's Salt Lake City Beers		.20
Pabst Export		.20
Schlitz Export		.20
Lemp's Extra Pale		.20
Anheuser-Busch Budweiser		.20
Club Soda, C. & C.		.25
Imported Ginger Ale, C. & C.		.25
Manitou Ginger Champagne		.25

		1-4 PT.	GLASS
LIQUORS, ETC.	Old Sherry, 1-2 Pint, 50		
	Walker's Canadian Club, 1-2 pt., 50	.40	.20
	Bourbon Whiskey	.40	.20
	Rye Whiskey	.40	.20
	Scotch Whiskey		.25
	Brandy	.50	.30
	Plymouth or Holland Gin	.40	.20
	Club Cocktails, Whiskey, Gin, Etc.		.20
	Creme de Menthe		.20
	Lemonade		.15

		PTS.
WATERS, ETC.	Manitou Water	.25
	Apollinaris Water	.25
	Hathorn Water	.25
	Hunyadi, Glass, 15; Bottle, 35.	
	Bromo Soda, Glass, 10; Bottle, 35.	

CIGARS Havana, Key West and Domestic, 10 each; 2 for 25; 15 each; 3 for 50; 25 each Cigarettes, Domestic, 15 and 20 per package; Imported, 15 per pkg. Playing Cards, 50 per pack.

MENU COURTESY C. A. WALL, D & RGW DINING CAR DEPT.

BREAKFAST

Menu

À LA CARTE

Strawberries and Cream, 20
Fresh Fruit, 15   Preserved Figs, 20

Cracked Wheat, with Cream, 20   Oat Meal, with Cream, 20

Coffee, per cup, 10   Coffee, per pot, 15
Milk, per glass, 10
Coffee, per pot, for two, 25   Cream, per glass, 15
English Breakfast or Green Tea, per pot, 15.. per pot, for two, 25
Chocolate or Cocoa, with Whipped Cream, per cup, 15

Celery, 15   Cucumbers, 15   Sliced Tomatoes, 15

Broiled White Fish, 35   Broiled or Boiled Salt Mackerel, 35
Mountain Trout in season,   Codfish Balls, 30

Tenderloin Steak, 50   Sirloin Steak, 60
Extra Sirloin Steak, for two, 1.00
Spring Chicken, whole, 85; half, 50   Lamb Chops, 45
Mutton Chops, 40   Bacon (full order), 35
Broiled or Fried Ham, 35   Veal Cutlet, plain or breaded, 40
Ham and Eggs, 50   Calf's Liver and Bacon, 40
Bacon and Eggs, 40

WITH ABOVE ORDERS (EXTRA)
Mushrooms or French Peas, 15   Tomato Sauce, 10
Rasher of Bacon, 10

EGGS
Boiled, Fried, Scrambled, Shirred, 20   Plain Omelet, 20
Poached, on Toast, 30   Ham, Cheese, or Jelly Omelet, 30
Spanish or Mushroom Omelet, 35

POTATOES
Baked or French Fried, 10   Lyonnaise, 15
Hashed Brown, 15   German Fried, 15   Au Gratin, 15

Hot Rolls, 10   Corn Muffins, 10   Dry Toast, 10   Milk Toast, 15
Buttered Toast, 10   Cream Toast, 25
Wheat Cakes, with Maple Syrup, 20

Bread, butter and French fried or baked potatoes served with meat or fish orders without extra charge.

No order taken or check issued for a less amount than 25 cents for each person. A charge of 25 cents is made for each extra person served from a single meat or fish order.

Service by waiter outside of dining car, 25 cents extra for each person served.

This Menu May Be Retained as a Souvenir

FRED JUKES

Winter at Cumbres in 1909 found Fred Jukes, an old-time boomer, on hand with a camera to record the scene on the ready track with a triple-headed freight waiting its turn at the water spout after two passenger engines get their fill. Not so very different, allowing for a change of seasons, is a summer view of the roundhouse at Salida in 1882 as three narrow gauge ponies with faithful Towser in the foreground pose for their portrait by some now unknown photographer.

JACKSON THODE COLLECTION

RICHARD KINDIG COLLECTION

Winter in Leadville, 1905, found four engines and a flanger in a truly mixed consist with four coaches, an ore car and a flanger. BELOW: Two narrow gauge yard engines flank a standard goat at Pueblo to show the three-fold coupling arrangements that prevailed as long as there was mixed operation.

WESTERN COLLECTION

More than half a century ago, Fred Jukes, who today lives in Blaine, Washington, was a boomer railroader with a sure conviction that the railroad scene was changing and that a pictorial dossier would one day be valuable as part of the record of the Old West. He patiently photographed hundreds of scenes, from the Canadian border to the Rio Grande, of trains in action, roundhouses, operations, installations, personnel and rolling stock, and on these and the two following pages and scattered elsewhere throughout this volume are presented some of Fred Jukes prints of Colorado narrow gauges in a day of diamond stacks and link-and-pin couplings on some of the older equipment.

On this page No. 404 poses for a glowing likeness at Sargents Station in 1902, before automatic couplers were ever known on Marshall Pass, while (BELOW) a double-header seen from atop a carload of milled lumber heads out onto the trestle at Lobato. On the page opposite, No. 206 poses at Table Rock to show its automatic couplers and two link-and-pin sockets for handling cars on a three-rail track and (BELOW) a brace of diamond stacks in tandem at Chama are on the ready track to roll westward to Durango with a redball merchandise.

FOUR PHOTOS: FRED JUKES

A Garland For Old Times by Fred Jukes

In 1908 the Rio Grande engine house at Chama, division point on the run between Alamosa and Durango, was a forest of diamond stacks clustered against a background of rolling Colorado mountains. Twenty-five years later, the Colorado & Southern's No. 9 on the old South Park paused briefly on the Denver-Leadville run to set out light merchandise at the summit of Boreas Pass, 11,493 feet above sea level.

The year was 1907 when the D&RGW engine No. 206 (PAGE OPPOSITE) and its crew posed for posterity on the drawbar in Rock Cut west of Chama, while (AT RIGHT) the day passenger run of the same year and before the train was formally known as *The San Juan* passes the photographer on the hill between Chama and Cumbres as a courtly passenger on the platform doffs his hard hat.

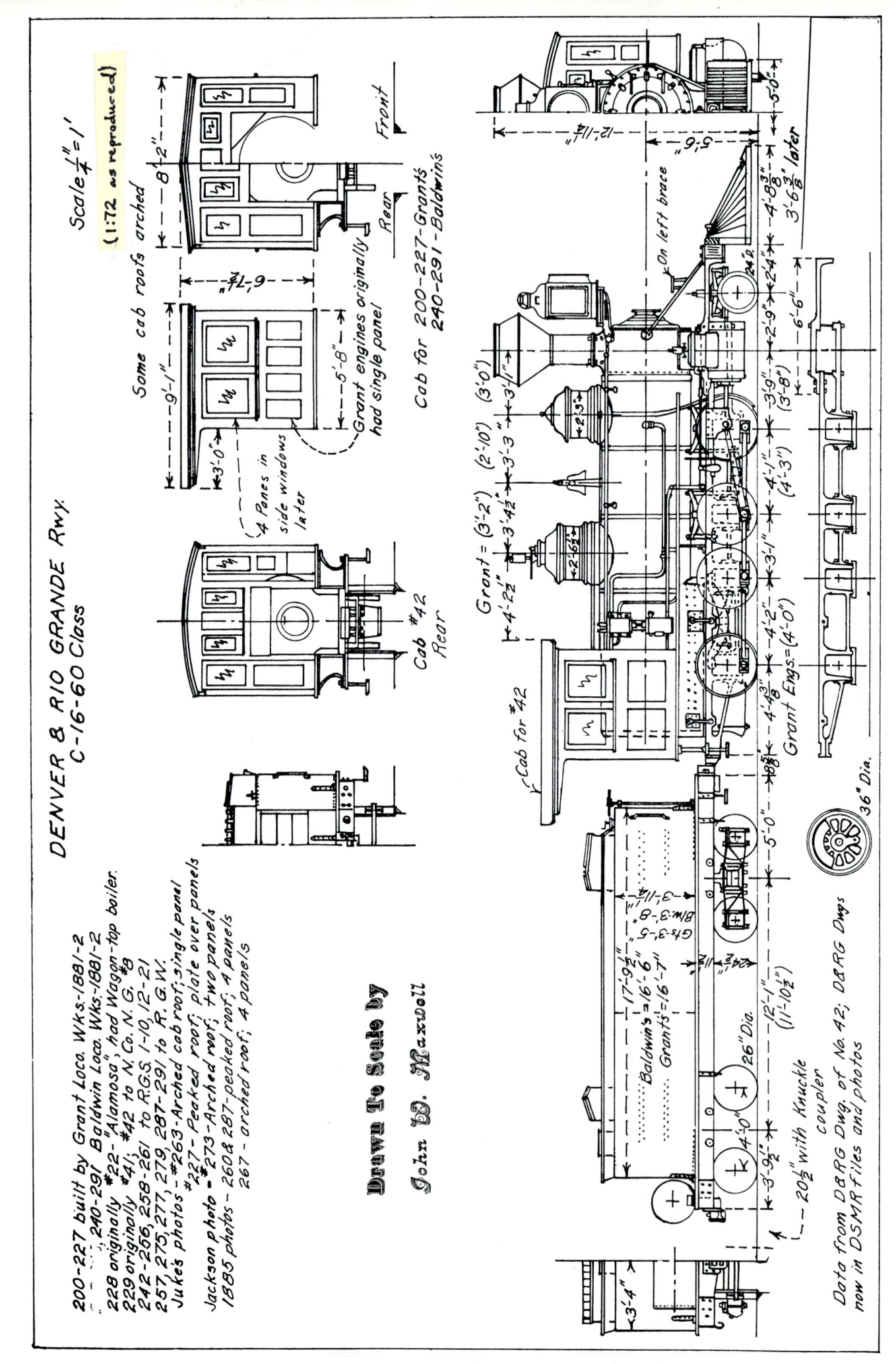

One of the greatest old-time photographs ever exposed of the railroads of an earlier West was taken back in 1907 by Fred Jukes. It shows a triple-header on the narrow gauge D&RGW headed by No. 419 as it breasted the grade out of Chama on the Alamosa to Durango mainline of the pioneer carrier. ABOVE: The smokebox of No. 478, in recent years assigned to the Silverton train out of Durango, as it stood in Durango yards in 1957, while on the page opposite is a builder's elevation of one of the D&RGW's Grant-built Class C-16-60 ten-wheelers. Before the abandonment of passenger service between Alamosa and Durango No. 478 was often to be seen on the business end of *The San Juan* of fond memory, and an action photograph of it on this happy errand is available elsewhere in this volume.

JIM SHAUGHNESSY

FRED JUKES

FRED JUKES

CHARLES CLEGG

The San Juan

Back in 1905, as shown in the photograph on the page opposite, the day train between Durango and Alamosa that later became *The San Juan* was known in the region it served as *The Colorado & New Mexico Express* and carried a through parlor car from Silverton. A 2-8-0 and a ten-wheeler, one with diamond and one with a straight stack, were needed to get the diminutive varnish over the hill at Chama. Forty years later *The San Juan*, depicted on this page climbing the grade out of Durango in 1946, had much the same consist, and its parlor-observation car *Durango*, shown on the page opposite pausing at Dulce, boasted in addition to its reserved seats and open platform a restaurant compartment with light collations served by a steward who had once been in the service of Samuel Vauclain.

CHARLES CLEGG

JOHN W. MAXWELL   WESTERN COLLECTION

LUCIUS BEEBE

In the summer of 1941 the Denver & Rio Grande Western's train No. 315 with No. 346 on the smoky end, paused for this photograph by Gerald M. Best. It exemplified narrow gauge railroading in the grand manner as it waited at Cimarron for its eastbound opposite on the Montrose-Salida run. Weathered water tank, engineer oiling his valve motion, lounging crew and expectant passengers against the timeless Colorado hills are remnants of a vanished but wonderful way of life.

GERALD M. BEST

"The Camp Bird was producing $5,000 a day. Each morning we Walshes arose richer than when we had gone to bed," wrote Evalyn Walsh McLean years later in *Father Struck It Rich*. Nine miles from Ouray, the Camp Bird Mine was one of the fabled producers of the Old West. The wealth of grizzled old Tom Walsh, the one-time hotel keeper of Leadville, became one of the legendary American fortunes. One beneficiary was Leopold, King of the Belgians, a close friend of the Ouray archmillionaire. Wearing the Hope diamond, Evalyn Walsh McLean became the most spectacular hostess in the history of Washington. Her first child was known as "The Hundred Million Dollar Baby." President Harding was her close friend and confidant; her entertainments staggered the imagination of crowned heads. From the Camp Bird, on the page opposite, came an almost limitless torrent of wealth and it was easy to see why Otto Mears thought Ouray needed a direct railroad connection with the outer world. It got it but not through the agency of Mears. PAGE OPPOSITE: The Denver & Rio Grande Western's 2-8-0 No. 340 on the Armstrong turntable at the end of Box Canyon at Ouray in 1951.

LUCIUS BEEBE

LUCIUS BEEBE

The beautiful Victorian facade of the Grand Imperial Hotel at Silverton maintains the illusion, evoked by the narrow gauge, of miners in jackboots and nabobs in frock coats and Albert watch chains moving in a pageant of silver destinies against the incomparable backdrop of Anvil Mountain, when all the world was young. BELOW: the view from the car platforms down Animas Canyon recalls the remark of the timid lady traveler in primeval times who, seeing an uncommonly fat man in an outside seat, asked him if he would mind leaning a little toward the center of the car until it had rounded the curve.

62

Back in the wartime years of 1944 and 1945 and before it was one of the great tourist attractions of Colorado, the Silverton train ran on a slender twice-a-week schedule with a single combine and caboose at the end of its mixed consist. It is shown below crossing the highway north of Durango before essaying the grade upward toward Rockwood. In the above photograph the same train is depicted a few miles farthur on its run, passing through a winter stand of hemlock with snow on its great iron wedge plow to show where the tracks have been hidden by blowing drifts.

LUCIUS BEEBE

CHARLES CLEGG

FRED JUKES   JIM SHAUGHNESSY

In the half-century that had elapsed between the time Fred Jukes took this matchless classic of early narrow gauge operations on the D & RG in 1907, and the year 1957, when Jim Shaughnessy took the ponderous shot of narrow gauge running gear shown on the page opposite, the operations of the three-foot road had come a far piece. As elsewhere in the world of railroading, motive power on the narrow gauge came closest to perfection as it stood on the brink of dissolution. On this page (BELOW) the D&RGW's Consolidation No. 268 rolls off a trestle on the Gunnison branch near Sapinero in a fancy paint job with which it had recently been invested to participate in the filming of a cinema Western, while (ABOVE) the fireboy leans out of the cab of No. 482 into the hot Colorado darkness while awaiting a highball to take off with an eastbound manifest in Durango yards.

JIM SHAUGHNESSY

JOHNNY KRAUSE

The recovery of precious metals from the deep mines of Colorado and their reduction in such stamp mills as that shown at the left was the impetus that built narrow gauge lines into the inaccessible pockets of the Rockies, the San Juans and the Uncompahgre Mountains. On the flood tide of mining in the eighties the narrow gauges prospered; in recurrent recessions of mining the railroads, too, operated in borrasca. As mines were closed and mining towns turned to ghost towns, so also were the three-foot rails torn up, their rights of way abandoned, their once populous traffickings relegated to the realm of wistful memories of a golden time. BELOW: an ore train of the D & RGW, behind No. 318, trailing a noble cloud of exhaust smoke rolls out onto one of the numerous trestles of the Ouray run. On the page opposite, *The Shavano*, last but one of the narrow gauge name trains to operate in passenger service, is pictured in its final days in a print processed by Fred Jukes from a negative by Otto Perry. The little varnish train was assigned to the run between Gunnison and Salida as No. 315 and 316 and its twin observation cars, *Salida* and *Gunnison*, were known for their extra large platforms and deep, comfortable armchairs inside.

JOHNNY KRAUSE

OTTO PERRY

CHARLES CLEGG

Railroad operating departments in the age of steam did not always see eye-to-eye with railroad buffs or share the sentiments of rail-photographers in the matter of smoke and steam exhaust. Firemen were encouraged to an economical use of fuel and a clean fire which showed a minimum of smoke whereas photographers wanted a pillar of cloud suggesting a major conflagration in progress. When veteran Colorado photographer Otto Perry encountered the Rio Grande's No. 318 leaving the Black Canyon of the Gunnison against a background of gathering thunderclouds one summer's afternoon, the operating department's edict against excessive smoke was in full effect. BELOW: No. 452 splashes water into its tank in Durango yards preparatory to heading east toward Chama with a string of merchandise in the closing year of the 1941 war. A cliche and stock shot of the railroad photographer, taking water, never lost its fascination for the beholder as long as steam dominated the carriers and was the only motive power acknowledged by The Faithful.

On September 23, 1909, the President of the United States, William Howard Taft, came to Colorado to press a gold pushbutton set in a silver plate that would signal the opening of the great Gunnison Tunnel, one of the irrigation projects on a large scale of the Federal Reclamation Bureau. Accompanied by a bodyguard of Colorado sheriffs and civic dignitaries, the President boarded the narrow gauge special shown here at Salida for the trip over Marshall Pass to Gunnison. As he weighed at the time upward of twenty stone, there was some speculation as to whether narrow gauge equipment could handle the tonnage and a special chair was installed in a narrow gauge business car to accommodate the ample presidential beam. Here the Presidential Special is shown ready to take off from Salida depot, No. 168 specially furbished for the occasion, bunting draped, and the eagle-eye wearing a hard derby hat, the hat (not the Stetson) that won the West. Although the presidential progress to Gunnison was without incident, as much could not be said for his stay in Denver. Anxious to experience the true feeling of Colorado's storied yesterdays, President Taft attempted to take a bath in the celebrated tin tub in the Windsor Hotel, for the filling of which, when Baby Doe wanted to take a bath, H. A. W. Tabor used to fee bellhops at the rate of a dollar a bucket in a time before piped water. The presidential aft became fast wedged in the narrow confines of the bath and heroic measures, including a deal of soaping and pulling by the management, were necessary to extricate him.

FRED JUKES COLLECTION

OTTO PERRY

The Chili Line, as the run between Antonito and Santa Fe was known by reason of the quantities of chili beans cultivated by the Spanish residents along its right of way, was a branch line operation of little traffic and great scenic and atmospheric charm. Its right of way, at one time when the Rio Grande had been denied access to the Cajon, was briefly considered as a bypass between Denver and New Mexico on the way to the Mexican border and for miles ran beside the Rio Grande of the railroad's corporate title. At Barranca Hill there was a four per cent grade which veteran engineers treated with extreme respect and the entire length of the run was made through a region where the Spanish heritage lay heavily on society, speech and architecture. The Chili train north from Santa Fe and south from Antonito usually consisted of a coach and one or two baggage and mail cars. Between Antonito and Alamosa it was customarily a part of the *San Juan* until 1941, when the railroad obtained permission from the ICC to abandon and the Chili Line became one more souvenir in the book of narrow gauge memories. The fantastic rise of tourism in the American West in the years following the 1941 war has frequently given rise to speculation as to what might have been the traffic over the romantic and atmospheric Chili route had it continued in operation a decade longer. A ride over the narrow gauge to Santa Fe would certainly have been comparable in tourist appeal to the Silverton run that proved so unexpectedly popular and, indeed, actually profitable.

OTTO PERRY

In a countryside largely barren of potable water, the Rio Grande's Chili Line performed as a public utility in more ways than one, hauling water in tank cars for distribution at strategic points along the right of way. Here one of these is spotted at Taos Junction while a horse-drawn water cart right out of any mining town in the seventies pauses to allow its owner to negotiate a drink for himself. BELOW is shown No. 473 with the Chili train, No. 425, on the trestle across the Rio Grande itself just below San Ildefonso. The date is July, 1940, as the sands in the glass are running out for one of the most picturesque of all the Rio Grande's narrow gauge operations.

RICHARD B. JACKSON

OTTO PERRY

In the top photograph No. 473 is shown southbound out of Antonito on the Santa Fe run at the junction where the Santa Fe branch meets the three track line to Alamosa and the narrow gauge mainline to Chama and Durango. Late in the afternoon the northbound section of the same train was carded to coincide with the arrival at Antonito of *The San Juan* from the west and the combined trains, as shown below, then ran in a single consist behind No. 470 for the remaining miles to Alamosa.

RICHARD B. JACKSON

CARL FALLBURG

In a land so predominantly Spanish in its origins that wash rooms are marked *hombres* and *mujeres,* it was only appropriate that the ice-water tanks on the coaches assigned to the Chili run as well as those on the Alamosa-Durango trains should be identified bilingually. In the below photograph, the Chili train stops also for a drink at Rio Grande water tower just before the track turned north and crossed the river to run up to San Ildefonso. In 1919, the tank stop was also listed as Rio Grande Station, but by the time this picture was taken the stop had vanished from the timetable of the year 1940. It was, in reality, the Chili run to Santa Fe that lent justification to the inclusion of Rio Grande in the corporate title of the railroad, and when service over it was finally abandoned, the name of the Denver & Rio Grande Western was as spurious as any of the hundred hopeful railroads whose names ended in "& Pacific" but never got there. Because of its thronging historical associations at the Santa Fe end of the line, the Chili run's memory is still green in the minds of students of the Southwest's legendary yesterdays. Its disused right of way is haunted by the ghosts of Kit Carson and all the Mountain Men and the Long Hunters who made the Santa Fe Trail, Bent's Fort on the Arkansas and the old pueblo at Taos names starred in the long tally of romantic places in the nation's annals.

JOHN W. MAXWELL

Gloomy were the winter skies on Christmas eve of 1940 at Santa Fe, as an end loomed forever of operations over the Chili Line between Santa Fe and Antonito over the narrow gauge.

LUCIUS BEEBE

LUCIUS BEEBE

OTTO PERRY

A landmark for many years along the Chili Line was this fifty-foot turntable at Embudo, New Mexico, shaded in proper season with cottonwoods and manually operated by train crews requiring its service. In the frame below, No. 473 easily rolls the Chili train beside the Rio Grande of the railroad's name near Otowi in the last year of operations over the branch.

OTTO PERRY

FRED JUKES

OTTO PERRY

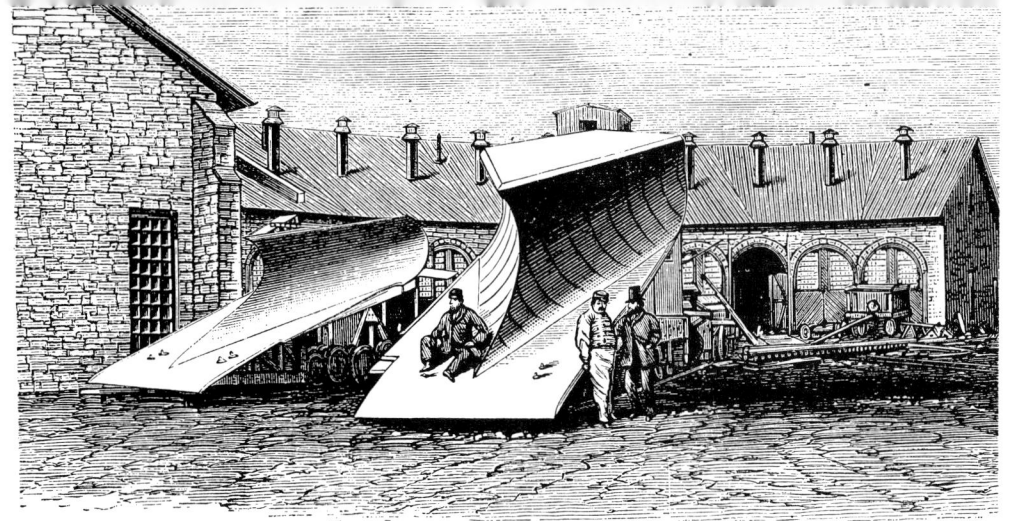

OTTO PERRY

Since its first operations, snow has been a factor in Rio Grande thinking and economy, as shown by the photograph at the top of the page opposite taken more than fifty years ago at Cumbres by Fred Jukes. BELOW: In 1940, No. 360, an ex-Crystal River 2-8-0, and No. 454 and 361 westbound, start the four-and-a-half per cent grade up Cerro Summit out of Cimarron for Montrose, while on this page the same train heads into the winter landscape for a pastoral of steam and snow and steel.

EDGAR T. MEADE

OTTO PERRY

ROBERT HALE

On a bright September morning (PAGE OPPOSITE) the Rio Grande's veteran No. 361 is depicted in 1942, half a mile west of Gunnison town with a consist of stock cars destined for Montrose and eventually interchange with the Rio Grande Southern for cattle movement from the ranges of Dolores and Mancos. The Marshall Pass line over the narrow gauge to the markets of Denver was for many years favored by shippers of sheep at Placerville, largest shipping point in the entire state of Colorado, over the standard gauge via the Dotsero Cutoff. The route was more expeditious; sheep were less crowded in narrow gauge stock cars and fetched higher prices at Denver stockyards. With the closing of the Marshall Pass route, much of the ancient glory departed the narrow gauge and the loss of its shipping facilities alienated the sympathies of thousands of ranchers and farmers along the once populous transcontinental link. In the upper frame, ten-wheeler No. 278 gleams fresh from the paint shop on the Gunnison turntable. On this page, the big time and mainline implications of the narrow gauge are captured in a revealing photograph by Robert Hale taken in Alamosa yards where wedge plows, smokeboxes, coupling knuckles and a glimpse of old-time wooden coaches in the background are blended in a montage of the essence of railroading.

PHOTO ROBERT RICHARDSON; PRINT CHARLES CLEGG

LUCIUS BEEBE

The D & RGW's narrow gauge flanger on a siding at Durango is massively built with a solid steel frame and power activated butterflies, with an eye to the heavy duty when winter comes to Animas or the mainline above Chama. At the top of the page, No. 476 and 484, double-headed, thunder magnificently across the Conejos River on the run between Alamosa and Cumbres for an immortal portrait of the merchandise rolling into the sunset down the three-foot rails.

The fifty-odd miles of tangent on the San Luis Valley line of the D&RGW between Alamosa and Salida, like the line itself, is now only a memory, but once it was crowded with freight traffic and at the turn of the century it was an integral part of the Narrow Gauge Circle. Here the last train with two high cars of merchandise runs up the San Luis Valley in February, 1951, against a dark background of winter sky and the snow-covered Sangre de Cristos. At the left is what must have been one of the earliest of all narrow gauge action photographs, since the stereoptican slide from which it was lifted bore the date 1889. It shows a double-header on the run between Antonito and Chama but no further detail or identification of the photographer who exposed his wet plate on that now distant day.

OTTO PERRY COLLECTION

ROBERT W. RICHARDSON

R. W. RICHARDSON COLLECTION

GORDON S. CROWELL

JACKSON THODE

When the D & RGW's depot at Alamosa burned in 1912, it was a very stylish conflagration indeed, as is evidenced by the presence of representatives of the county families in riding boots and well-cut jackets. Shortly after this photograph was taken, the roof fell in and the railroad set about building a new station which stands to this day. In the picture on the same page, a double-headed merchandise run out of Alamosa occupies the narrow gauge iron of a three-rail track which even now spans the distance from Alamosa to Antonito, where once the Chili line took off for Santa Fe and where the three-foot rails still head west for Chama and Durango. On this page, in the last year of operations over the Salida to Monrose run via Gunnison and the Black Canyon that had once been the Rio Grande's transcontinental mainline, No. 454 tops the four per cent grade at Cerro Summit west of Cimarron for a vista of steam railroading in microcosm against the backdrop of the Colorado hills.

At the bottom of this page, No. 483 fitted with a wedge plow drowses away the dark hours on the ready track at Salida in an aura of enginehouse warmth and light, while in the above frame, it joins the morning line-up of narrow gauge motive power for Monarch as, at the left, a standard gauge 2-8-0 stands by for working the yards. On the page opposite is the Crested Butte depot in 1888, with the station agent posing with his family, both official and personal, for a rendezvous with celluloid immortality. At the bottom of the page, while the sun sets prophetically over the Valley of the Gunnison, a night freight heads up the grade toward Marshall Pass for a remarkably atmospheric photograph taken from the caboose by James M. Morley. This is the twilight of the narrow gauge, Gotterdammerung for the gods of steam.

TWO PHOTOS: JIM SHAUGHNESSY

WESTERN COLLECTION

JAMES M. MORLEY

The first Pullman car *Alamosa*, whose interior and exterior are shown on this page, was delivered for service on the daily run between Durango and Alamosa as equipment for the *San Juan Express* in 1904, and some idea of its splendors of Pintsch lighting system, red plush individual seats and generally luxurious *decor* may be gained from this rare photograph from the collection of John W. Maxwell. The first *Alamosa* survived in service until 1917, when it was wrecked and burned. Two exactly similar cars, the *Durango* and the *Silverton*, eventually became part of the *Shavano* on the Gunnison run, where they were known as *Salida* and *Gunnison*, respectively. This was the second car to be named *Durango*, as the first, like the *Alamosa,* had been destroyed by wreck and fire in 1910. A glory rode the narrow gauge and much of it was expressed in plate glass, burled walnut and silver-finished coal oil lamps in a profusion to delight the customers and permit the carriers to point with uncommon pride. On the page opposite, *The San Juan,* double-headed and with six head-end revenue cars at Windy Point in 1937 is the realization of a railroad photographer's dream achieved by Richard B. Jackson.

PAGE OPPOSITE: RICHARD B. JACKSON

TWO PHOTOS: JOHN W. MAXWELL COLLECTION

LUCIUS BEEBE

JACKSON C. THODE

In the days when the narrow gauge capital of the universe was Durango, its yards were the Mecca of the faithful to whom railroading is a major preoccupation regardless of hour or season. On the page opposite, No. 491 greets a July dawn with the coal tipple for a background at the top, while (BELOW) No. 472 prepares to depart from Durango depot with *The San Juan* after a light fall of snow. On this page, No. 478 is serviced for the Silverton run on the morrow and (BELOW), it slumbers against a morning call to power the last regularly scheduled narrow gauge passenger train in the United States. In the summer months of 1957 alone the Silverton train carried 25,000 passengers on the round trip up the Canyon of Animas for a gross revenue to the railroad in excess of $100,000 and immeasurably stimulated the economies of its terminals at Durango and Silverton where hotels, restaurants and tourism generally thrived on the excursionists attracted by the romantic narrow gauge.

TWO PHOTOS: JIM SHAUGHNESSY

NIGHT OVER DURANGO

By Jim Shaughnessy

The pastoral quality of back country railroading in the Colorado uplands is suggested by cattle guards in the mountain meadows above Rockwood on the Silverton run. BELOW: No. 478 awaits the highball in Durango to take the Silverton train away, with the water bag on the fireman's side characteristic of all narrow gauge assignments during the hot Colorado summer.

LUCIUS BEEBE

JIM SHAUGHNESSY

Although narrow gauge passenger operations in the United States were widespread and reached from Down East Maine to the Blue Mountains of Oregon and from Michigan to Owens Valley in California, nowhere did they lend so special a character to the landscape they traversed and the communities they served as in Colorado. Here their identification was complete with every aspect of regional life and regional economy. Colorado's ample destinies rode the three-foot cars in a special aura of diminutive romance and the impact of their operations was felt everywhere from the Front Range to the Utah line and beyond. Here, near Romeo south of Alamosa, No. 487, a well-shopped 2-8-2, shows its heels on the smoky end of *The San Juan* in the closing years of its operations. The automobile might supplant, aye even eliminate the iron pony, but the Colorado heart will be aware of the narrow gauge and steam locomotives forever.

JIM SHAUGHNESSY

WESTERN COLLECTION

The Mears Short Lines

Although as much could not always have been said for its early scuffles with geography, by 1882 the Denver & Rio Grande Railroad knew with some degree of assurance where it was going. It arrived in Silverton up the spectacular Canyon of Animas from Durango in that year, whereupon its engineers took a look at the formidable peaks of the Uncompahgre Mountains surrounding every side except the pass through which the river vented the *cul-de-sac* of Baker's Park in which Silverton is located, and said that was as far as they were going. Anyone desirous of continuing to Ouray or Telluride could board the stages and arrive over Otto Mears's Rainbow Toll Road. Nobody was ever going to get to Ouray from the south by rail.

The Rio Grande was not altogether right in this forecast and in time the steamcars were going to achieve Ouray over the Rio Grande's own rails, and from Silverton, too, if you wanted to figure it that way, but by such indirection as nobody could have foreseen in 1882.

By this time, however, Otto Mears had been thoroughly infected with the contagion of railroading. On every hand his toll roads were being tracked for the engines and cars. Ouray and Telluride were booming in wildest frenzies of bonanza and if the Rio Grande would not build a route there out of Silverton, he, Mears, would be agreeable to showing them how. It was only twenty-six miles after all.

The result, five years later in 1887, was the Silverton Railroad, a narrow gauge carrier not only remarkable for its determined projection and alarming profile, but also for the promotional overtones which lent it a celebrity beyond all deserving of its eighteen miles of track from nowhere to practically nowhere.

One of the interesting things about Mears was that seemingly he could always come up with financial backing proportionate to the Mears enthusiasm, which was considerable. Mears could bluff, too, and effectively. Back in 1873, he had won rate concessions from the Rio Grande Railroad while freighting out of Saguache with three teams by threatening to establish a rival ox-team service. But now he came up with better than $700,000 hard cash and the Silverton Railroad started north with the dirt flying from the shovels of grading crews. It followed the course of Mineral Creek to Chattanooga, then rounded a sharp hairpin curve on the way to the summit, the top of Red Mountain Pass with an elevation of 11,235 feet. Beyond the pass, the line descended to Red Mountain town, Guston, and Ironton via a bewilderment of loops and switchbacks, including the fantastic arrangement of trackage in Corkscrew Gulch which included both a switchback and the celebrated covered turntable.

Within a year of its incorporation, the Silverton Railroad was in business on a scale gratifying in the extreme to its promoters and arousing a mild degree of envy in Rio Grande breasts. Two trains a day were running from Silverton to Red Mountain town and return at twenty cents a passenger mile, with no abatement for round-trip tickets, infants or other deadheads. Its little cars, jammed to the platforms with miners headed to See The Elephant in Silverton, were a very profitable proposition indeed. These were the days when mainline railroads figured that any passenger train grossing a dollar a mile for its operation was showing a profit and, with two cars filled with paying customers to a run, Mears was grossing twenty dollars a mile. Things along the Silverton were looking up.

Although the Red Mountain district had been in existence since the late seventies and from Silverton to Chattanooga and thence to Red Mountain Pass, along Mears's toll road there had been an almost continuous chain of mines. Red Mountain's golden noontide of production and wealth flowered with the coming of the Silverton Railroad in 1888.

Red Mountain town itself had at first been located farther down the mountainside but when Slover & Wright erected their new and handsome saloon up the slope a way to escape snowslides, the town naturally followed, even against gravity, and relocated itself handy to this paragon of oasis, "which would be an honor and credit to a town much larger than ours."

The Solid Muldoon, Dave Day's terrible-tempered Ouray paper, commented, "Five weeks ago, where Red Mountain now stands was a woodland mesa covered with heavy spruce timber. Today, hotels, printing offices, groceries, meat markets, a telephone office, saloons and dance houses are up and booming; the blast is heard on every side and prospectors can be seen snowshoeing in every direction." There was talk of a water works and other metropolitan airs.

As the railroad approached, Red Mountain and Ironton began to run a perceptible fever.

"It has been casually suggested that when the graders begin moving dirt through Red Mountain, a day be set apart by a number of our citizens and leisure-

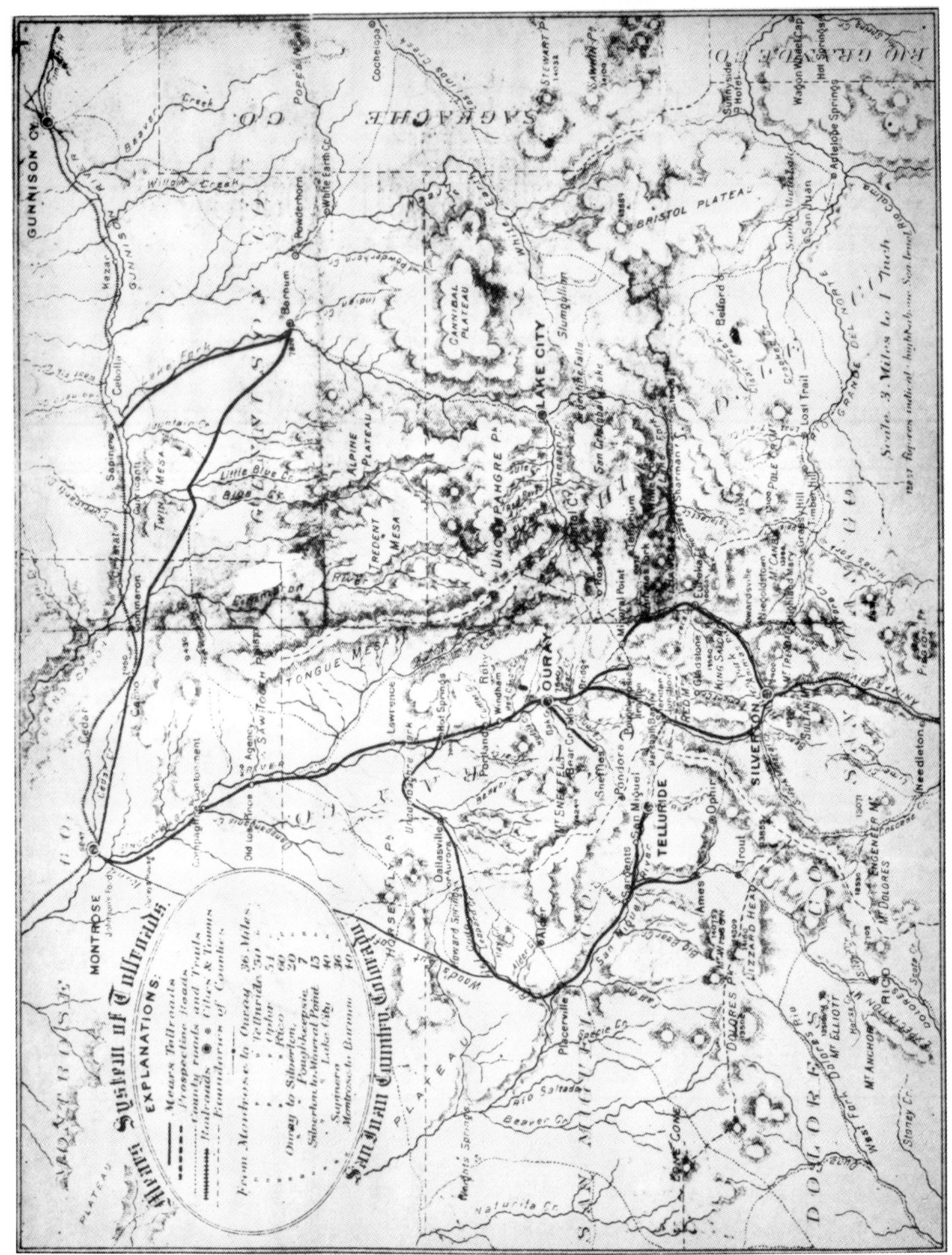

RICHARD KINDIG COLLECTION

hour people and that they make 500 feet of grade for the railroad," said *The Red Mountain Mining Journal*, one of the town's improbable three newspapers. "At the same time we should arrange to have a silver spike driven in the most central part of the track. The people of Chattanooga are going to have a ball; the people of Silverton, at the instigation of the Jockey Club, raised $500 to celebrate the first train down Red Mountain. Now we must most certainly do something to show our appreciation of the coming event. The graders are now between Chattanooga and Old Congress Town."

A wild surge of prosperity now engulfed Red Mountain. Between 20,000 and 30,000 tons of rich ore were carried out of the district annually over the narrow gauge, "receiving its silvery traffic from the realms of eternal snow," as the *Silverton Weekly Miner* remarked in a fine moment of poetry. Armed guards rode the Silverton's ore trains all the way down to the smelters at Durango and a total of $8,000,000 was recovered from the Yankee Girl alone in its best years. Other mines in the district and at Ironton produced better than $30,000,000. With a single-mine payroll of 2,300 men weekly, boom times came to Red Mountain. The railroad was hard put to bring in all the coal, whisky, and rubber boots the population required, and the loud, cheerful sounds of saloon life never died in the town's main drag. Proprietors of the numerous fandango houses established expensive connections in Denver's Holliday Street and the girls rode in first class aboard one of the railroad's two coaches. When there was a dance of the Knights of Labor or the Free Coinage Dancing Club, the Silverton's facilities were taxed and a boxcar was swept clean of ore traces and seats set inside. "The supper was uncommonly beautiful . . . confections were furnished by the Vienna Bakery of Ouray."

Otto Mears liked to think that one of these days the French pastry from the Vienna Bakery could arrive from Ouray on the steamcars instead of aboard the mail stage as was now the case.

Winters, which came early in the mountains and stayed late, were a trial. Service on the Silverton was intermittent and often the mine bosses called off operations underground to set their men to digging out the tracks so that the necessities of life, whisky, and women could get up the hill. The high-grade ore piled up in huge dumps that had to be guarded until spring or a chinook came along and made a cleanup possible.

An inspired promoter who could finance considerable ventures on no other security than his own native optimism, Mears understood the uses of publicity in an age when Madison Avenue was synonymous with brownstone residential respectability rather than renowned as the abode of hucksters, and he readily achieved newspaper space for his little railroads. His most celebrated gesture of publicizing for the Silverton road and one which was later used effectively when he had built the Rio Grande Southern, was an issuance of the Mears railroad passes which today are collectors' items that have provoked learned monographs among railroad historians.

Railroad passes of conventional design were the merest commonplace in the American eighties and nineties. Public officeholders, politicians, clergymen, play actors, legislators, newspapermen, important shippers, the families of railroad men and, indeed, anybody whose influence or friendship could be even remotely useful to the management, rode on passes. In time, the practice burgeoned into an abuse of nationwide proportions and eventually the Interstate Commerce Commission took steps for its abatement, but the latter years of the nineteenth century were the golden age of free-loading aboard the steamcars and it remained for Mears to give it a novel twist which brought fame and, in all probability, business to the Silverton run.

MORRIS ABBOTT COLLECTION

ROBERT RICHARDS

Even rarer than the Mears white buckskin pass over the Silverton Railroad—is this handsomely conceived solid silver special pass over the Rainbow Route suspended from a spoon of Red Mountain silver, designed to honor Mears as "Pathfinder of the San Juan." Both spoon and pass bear the conventional pattern of railroad tracks against a background of Colorado mountains beneath a symbolic rainbow, and the spoon is surmounted by a likeness of the old, bearded wagonmaster himself, appropriately cast in the silver of the region. This rare collector's item came into the possession of Morris W. Abbott, a specialist in the field of narrow gauge folklore, after prolonged correspondence through the agency of the *Rocky Mountain News* with a veteran resident of the San Juan region and is believed to be the only extant specimen. BELOW is the also very rare watch-fob pass, somewhat enlarged in reproduction.

Mears's first inspiration, in 1888, was the fabrication of passes over the Silverton that were engrossed on white buckskin instead of the conventional cardboard or bank-note paper affected by other carriers. The buckskin symbolized in a vague sort of way the wilderness through which the narrow gauge operated and, indeed, buckskin garments and similar artifacts have always been suggestive of the Mountain Men whose fringed attire was an occupational costume. Although difficult to engross and perishable in the extreme, the buckskin passes were a great success.

The following year, noting the mortality rate of the leather passes, Mears commissioned a Denver jeweler to run up passes in Colorado silver, which was also possessed of a regional association. It was, furthermore, durable and had a gratifying intrinsic value. The silver passes achieved an enviable reputation and holders became persons of modest distinction in the mountains. The silver tickets bore a scene of mountain railroading and the engraved signature of Mears, and in successive years, he varied their manufacture with a design in silver surrounded by delicate, open filigree work, passes in the form of watch fobs, and added a final and triumphant flourish to the whole business by bestowing elaborate gold filigree annual tickets to a select and favored few. Most of the recipients of the Mears passes were persons of purely local importance, but a number of authentic celebrities also received them, including George M. Pullman, Horace A. W. Tabor, Jay Gould, and David H. Moffat.

The number of these picturesque passes issued by the Pathfinder of the San Juan is today unknown, since he seems to have numbered them, not in logical sequence, but according to some private serial scheme all his own and never revealed. Students of the matter list their number at probably between fifty and one hundred. In any event, their promotional value was sufficient in Mears's judgment to carry the practice over to the operations of the Rio Grande Southern which, in large measure, was financed by the profitable Silverton road.

Encouraged by the success of the silver and gold passes, Mears went on to even greater schemes for promoting the fame of the Silverton's eighteen miles of thirty-five pound rails and set about providing the miners, who were currently paying twenty cents a passenger mile to ride the cars, with something in the form of luxury equipment. Until now passengers had been carried in primitive combines aboard which, according to David Lavender, the practice obtained of crowding the front seats on the way up the mountain and the rear space on the way down, to avoid the pools of tobacco juice which flooded the floor at whichever end of the conveyance was inclined downward at the moment.

The Silverton Railroad, whose entire distance was accomplished under ordinary operating conditions in less than two hours, needed a sleeping car about as much as it needed centralized traffic control or high-speed, roller-bearing trucks, but the idea appealed to Mears's sense of the preposterous and he set about providing not only sleeper service but club car and dining facilities as well, aboard a second-hand Pullman which the connecting Rio Grande Western had recently retired from the Salt Lake run which was now standard gauged.

The car was magnificent with red plush, solid silver trim, and the Eastlake decor favored of the period, and it immediately became a mark of worldly sophistication if not downright aristocratic achievement to have patronized the Silverton's splendid hotel car as it rolled in only slightly unsteady grandeur down the grade from Red Mountain and over the loops at Chattanooga. The sleeping accommodations which were retained at one end of the Pullman were occasionally put to

This hitherto unknown portrait of Otto Mears, a wash painting on board instead of conventional canvas, is one of the few available likenesses of the Wagon Master of the San Juan. It bears no date and the top hat was of a mode outdated shortly after the Civil War so that it affords no clue. It depicts Mears as a comparatively young man since by 1888, when known photographs of him exist, his beard was already streaked with gray. Colorado historians feel that the portrait, which is unsigned, may well have been painted in payment for some service by one of the itinerent artists of the time who made a living in the mining towns of the West executing commissions for business signs, saloon and music hall interiors and occasional portraits. The rare map on page 96 shows the Mears toll roads in the San Juan before The Pathfinder turned to railroading.

practical use when the little train became snowbound in winter months or was immobilized at Ironton or Albany by washouts on the line.

A local chronicler of the folklore of the Mears's lines has recorded that Otto's reclaimed sleeping-restaurant car comprised, in its inner economy, no fewer than four upper and four lower berths on each side of the center aisle, a ten-foot kitchen and twenty-foot dining compartment and lounge. Allowing six feet for the outside measurement of berths, these statistics would account for a car measuring no less than fifty-four feet exclusive of the depth of platforms at either end, but since the total length of the Rio Grande sleepers built by Pullman at his Detroit works was a scant forty-two feet from platform rail to platform rail, these proportions would seem a trifle optimistic. Lacking tangible evidence of more spacious dimensions, it is safe to say that the Silverton's palace hotel car, *Animas Forks*, included accommodations for sleeping, dining, and, assuredly, for drinking. Let us give no heed to the feet and inches involved.

Like much of the other rolling stock and motive power of the Silverton, the little Pullman was interchangeable in service over the Silverton Northern and the Gladstone run, and sometimes went as far into the great world as Durango over the connecting Rio Grande for the accommodation of a Boston banker or New York financier who might be interested in the mining opportunities of the region.

The *Animas Forks* set a style for diminutive varnish cars over the Mears's roads and a traffic in the business cars of executives of connecting roads and the slim gauge private cars of Colorado nabobs culminated, in 1917, in the arrival at Silverton, for an inspection tour of the Sunnyside zinc mines, of a group of Eastern capitalists who were considering the purchase of the property. The men of money, "seven of them millionaires", as an impressionable local reporter wrote, arrived aboard a solid train of narrow gauge varnish recruited from the business car pool of the Rio Grande, and so handsome was the entourage and so luxurious the appointments of the cars, that it remains a regional legend along with the Stoiber Mansion at Waldheim to this day.

On the way back from Eureka at the end of a week's entertainment of its important occupants, "The Millionaire's Special" was derailed and two of the beautiful cars burned when ignited from their Baker heaters. Despite this contretemps, the Eastern financiers were so favorably impressed that the Sunnyside sale was consummated and the mine passed into the hands of the United States Smelting & Refining Company.

Although an unqualified success as an agency of promotion and advertising for the railroad, the Silverton's Pullman was dogged with misfortune and so frequently was it overturned and otherwise damaged in minor accidents through the years that it was finally retired in the capacity of a summerhouse on the outskirts of Durango. "They say the lion and the lizard keep . . ."

Although it was eventually gathered into the Mears's network of narrow gauges, the Silverton, Gladstone & Northerly Railroad started life as a dream child of Cyrus W. Davis, president and a large stockholder in the Gold King Mine at Gladstone, and the Gold King properties were the important reason for the carrier's being. The Gold King was, in fact, a consolidation of some forty separate claims including the original Sampson Lode which had been operating on and off since 1882. Davis, a Down East Yankee from Waterville, Maine, felt that a railroad might put the whole Cement Creek mining setup on a paying basis and in 1899, the SG&N came into being.

There were five miles of drifts and tunnels in the Gold King and at the height of its productivity, it was shipping as many as 300 tons of concentrates daily to the Durango smelter. Its activities and that of the seven-and-a-half mile narrow gauge were all superintended from back East and the trustee was the Newtonville Trust Company of suburban Boston.

The SG&N commenced operations with two second-hand locomotives purchased from the Rio Grande and two homemade passenger and baggage combines, and there were at first two round trips between Silverton and Gladstone daily. A decade later, service had declined to a three-times-a-week mixed train in each direction and in the meantime, Otto Mears had leased the Gold King property and with it, the railroad, an arrangement which terminated when Mears and his partners acquired the entire business outright.

The annals of the SG&N were comparatively devoid of thrills, frills or moments of drama and exaltation. The days of the pioneers were passing when it came into being and the colorful passenger traffic in prospectors, gamblers, madames and other characters of bounce or outrage enjoyed by the other Colorado narrow gauges was almost altogether lacking.

In 1907, the short line enjoyed a brief experience of the limelight when a major conflagration destroyed the surface buildings at the mouth of the Gold King tunnel and a special train was chartered to bring rescue workers from Silverton as fast as the eagle eye could wheel his teapot locomotive over the light iron. "A hundred willing workers" arrived to take over, but not before six men were dead from the fumes. In 1915, service was permanently discontinued and two years later, Mears left Colorado. The annals of the Silverton, Gladstone & Northerly were short and simple and what romantic qualities can be assigned to its memory derive largely from the reflected glamor of its associated railroads and the remote and desolate character of the region of which it was a part.

When Muriel Wolle visited Gladstone in 1945, the town had ceased to exist.

In the closing years of the seventies, Otto Mears, in his capacity of wagon master of the San Juan and not infrequently as a speculator in mining properties of promise, had built one of his ubiquitous toll roads between Silverton and Mineral Point and on to Lake City following Animas to its forks, past what was to become the Silver Wing Mine at Eureka and the Gold Prince Mill at the Forks of Animas.

In 1889, as had been the case with so many of the Pathfinder's prudently surveyed and painstakingly graded toll roads, it became apparent that a feeder railroad from Silverton at least to Eureka would solve a lot of problems and what's more, that the most practicable route was already occupied by Mears's personal turnpike. "Put your line right down the wheel ruts," he told the surveyors. "I built the road; I guess I can lay track on it if I want to." Although part of the money to finance the narrow gauge came from the powerful Simon Guggenheim, progress was slow and the end of track only achieved Howardsville late in the year, when the *San Juan Democrat* remarked, "The Pathfinder's Iron Horse will shortly invade the tranquil precincts of Howardsville and Mayor Appel is preparing a speech which he will unload on the suffering but patient public."

The road never did get to Lake City and that community remained a Rio Grande monopoly untapped by the second greatest builder of narrow gauges, who sometimes functioned as opposition to the Palmer road and, at other times, was on the best of terms with the Denver monopoly. He was, for example, the only engineer who could be counted on to replace the Silverton branch of the Rio Grande when Animas rose and took its tracks, and the Rio Grande was glad to acknowledge his supremacy over this turbulent stream. Not all the elements bowed to the Pathfinder, however.

Witness the year 1906.

Mears accepted a contract from the Gold Prince Mill at Animas Forks which called for the transport of ore on a year-round basis, regardless of winter snows and spring freshets. Between the Forks and Eureka, where the most vicious snowslides were an annual occurrence, Mears designed snowsheds similar to but far more sturdy than those of his Rio Grande Southern at Lizard Head and comparable in their construction to the Central Pacific's celebrated storm shelters in the High Sierra. Solid walls of cribbing were "fortified with timbers of massive proportions lining each side of the track." At each end of the 500-foot structure were barracks where section hands were permanently housed, ready to leap into action with snow shovels and dynamite at the first sign of a blockade. Mears prayed for a truly terrific winter and promised that if his snowsheds proved their worth, the entire stretch of track from Eureka to Animas Forks would be under cover.

The elements took Mears at his word and a single slide wiped out his shed and his optimism at once. The all-weather contract with the Gold Prince was not renewed, nor did the railroad ever get to Mineral Point or Lake City.

More successful among Mears's skirmishes with the forces of nature and one which made him, if indeed that status had not already been attained, the grand old man of the Silverton region, was his triumph over Animas water in 1911, when the angry river made pretzels out of miles of rails in the narrowest part of Animas Canyon and Silverton was without communications with winter at hand. In desperation, Rio Grande officials wired to enlist Mears in the race against time, and the Pathfinder, then seventy, rushed reinforcements from his own railroads into the breach. Men and equipment from the Silverton railroads poured into the canyon. To keep the engines fired, coal was requisitioned from housewives and shopkeepers in Silverton although it was a fifty-fifty gamble. It was October and if winter set in before the trains were running again, Silverton would be a ghost town. The fuel was forthcoming, so great was the community's faith in Mears, and for nine weeks the track gangs and bridge builders strove mightily to replace the ravished rails.

A spectacle of heroic proportions, a diminutive, white-haired figure out of the ancestral past with his beard flying in the slipstream, was Otto Mears, his silk-hatted head thrust belligerently from a locomotive window as he drove up and down the tracks exhorting his legions to ever greater efforts. In the nick of time the last length of track was spiked into place and relief trains began running in from Durango with all the supplies for a long winter. As the first of their double-headed engines shouted its way through the cut at Rockwood, the heavens darkened and snow began to fall in the high passes. By night, the highways were out until April, but there was coal in the bins of Silverton and tinned stuff in the groceries, and in the bar of the Imperial Hotel and the Hub Saloon, where years before a drummer had been inspired to write words and music for "There'll be a Hot Time in the Old Town Tonight," Otto Mears's name was on every drink.

They didn't bury Otto Mears. When, a decade and a half later at the age of eighty-five, time at last caught up with the Pathfinder, his ashes were scattered high in the Uncompahgres above Silverton, where an old man could feel at home as he slept.

One of the amusing features of life along the Silverton Northern was a rail bicycle that Mears had had built for the pleasure and convenience of his friend, Mrs. Edward G. Stoiber, of Stoiber Waldheim near the Silver Lake Mine. The arrangement really was a handcar, on the framework of which, instead of the conventional handles with a sprocket connection to the axle, were two bicycles mounted so that a pair of riders could pedal the car as fast as eight or ten miles an hour without too much effort. Mrs. Stoiber and her friends often used the rail cycle to visit Silverton. Traffic was not so dense as to be dangerous. A possible cornfield meet could be averted when the smoke of No. 32 or 33 was discerned miles down the track and the trains were not fast enough to overtake the little car when it was going the other way.

The Silverton Northern had its pastoral moments, comparable to the Wildflower Trains on the beloved Colorado Midland and the Fish Trains in Platte Canyon on the South Park. Early in the century, according to Mrs. Josie Crum, a charitable event in Denver required a vast quantity of columbines, the official flower of Colorado, as decoration for its ballroom. Mears contributed a locomotive and train of flatcars, the crew donated its services and a local hardware dealer provided a quantity of washtubs. More than 25,000 columbines were gathered and sped to Denver over the Silverton Northern and the Rio Grande by special handling. When they got to the Queen City of the Plains, they were briefly displayed in front of the Champa Street office of the *Denver Post* where its proprietors, Harry Tammen and Fred Bonfils, who knew no shame in cutting themselves in on other people's promotion, managed to convey the impression that they had been responsible for the project.

From Eureka to Animas Forks, the grade was close to seven per cent, a hazard comparable to the seven-and-a-half per cent grade of the Uintah Railway at Morro Castle on the Colorado-Utah border. The road engine of the moment pushed the cars ahead of it to the Forks and then brought them down backwards while crews stood by the brakes with brake clubs at the ready. Two loaded freight cars up and three down was the limit handled on this section of track.

The backing down business was perilous and the legend persists in Colorado that in order to prevent accidents, Mears, in 1905, dismantled the roofed-in turntable at Corkscrew Gulch on the Silverton Railroad and moved it bodily to the Forks of Animas. This is an error which was finally disproved when a group of Colorado railroad historians which included Mac Poor, author of the epic *Denver, South Park & Pacific*, Ed Haley, Phil Ronfor, the artist, and Richard Kindig visited Corkscrew Gulch and found the turntable still there. They took a photograph to prove it, which is reproduced at an appropriate place in this chapter. The turntable at Forks of Animas on the Silverton Northern was of conventional design and neither roofed-in nor in any way protected from the elements as was the controversial structure on the Silverton road.

As with its fellow members of the Mears's narrow gauge family, the fortunes of the Silverton Northern rose as the mines operated in bonanza and declined when they achieved borrasca. Other mills and mines than the Gold Prince contributed to the railroad's fortunes: the Red Cloud at Mineral Point, the San Juan Chief, Polar Star, Syracuse Pride, Little Fraud, Bill Young and Annie Woods, most of which were located in the hills to the north of Animas Forks. And, of course, the great Sunnyside at Eureka and the Silver Wing.

The railroad never had more than four locomotives on its motive power roster at a single time, but as has been remarked before, motive power and rolling stock were interchangeable with the Silverton and the Silverton, Gladstone and Northerly, and it was difficult to tell who owned what at any given time.

Members of the Stoiber family died or moved away. Dust gathered in the fine ballroom of Stoiber Forest Home and the rare hocks in its cellars turned to vinegar. The engines of the Mears's roads rusted in disuse on the rip track at Silverton. Even slim and dainty No. 100, which had posed so proudly that morning for its portrait long ago at Treasure Tunnel, was scrapped. Ink more red than the Western slope of Red Mountain at sunset began appearing on the books of the Yankee Girl and the Guston, and long shadows fell across the entire region that the Mears's three-foot tracks had explored. Far away in the Federal City of Washington, Otto Mears was now an old man dreaming of epic bouts with the San Juan winters, the Animas when it had flooded its banks. The ties rotted and the rails spread on the three little railroads with the name Silverton in their corporate titles.

The Silverton Northern operated longest of all. As late as 1939, ore from the intermittently producing Sunnyside still went over the track in concentrate cars to Silverton. A miners' strike and the 1941 war put an end to all.

And finally, Otto Mears' toll road to Lake City, the golden turnpike to Golconda, reverted to its original state as a highway for wheeled vehicles that knew neither flange nor rail. The wheel had come full circle in the Uncompahgres.

WESTERN COLLECTION

On the morning of September 17, 1888—the date has been preserved on the original wet plate negative in the Western Collection—it was Otto Mears's whim to run a special excursion train out of Silverton to the end of track of his Silverton Railroad with a party of noteworthy guests. Among them was a photographer named T. M. McKee, who set up his ponderous camera by the right of way at Burro Bridge for this historic portrait of mountain railroading at its most rugged. Posed beside the pilot of No. 100 which had been optimistically named *Ouray*, is Mears himself, while his guests, in the fearful toggery of the time, survey his wilderness domain. At the top of the page, a pack train is being loaded at Red Mountain railhead for one of the remote mines of the region.

WESTERN COLLECTION

ABOVE is the same train whose front end is shown on the page opposite, with Otto Mears standing at the rear platform of the combine which he had stylishly named *Red Mountain*. Two open stages, one of whose drivers wears the ubiquitous derby, and a buckboard wait to carry Mears's party over the Toll Road to Ouray for a day's outing. BELOW: the Yankee Girl Mine, one of the great producers of the Red Mountain District, and the switchbacks of the Silverton Railroad by whose agency its two and three car trains were able to continue briefly around the mountainside to Ironton, but never, alas, to the Ouray of Mears's desire.

WILLIAM H. JACKSON: WESTERN COLLECTION

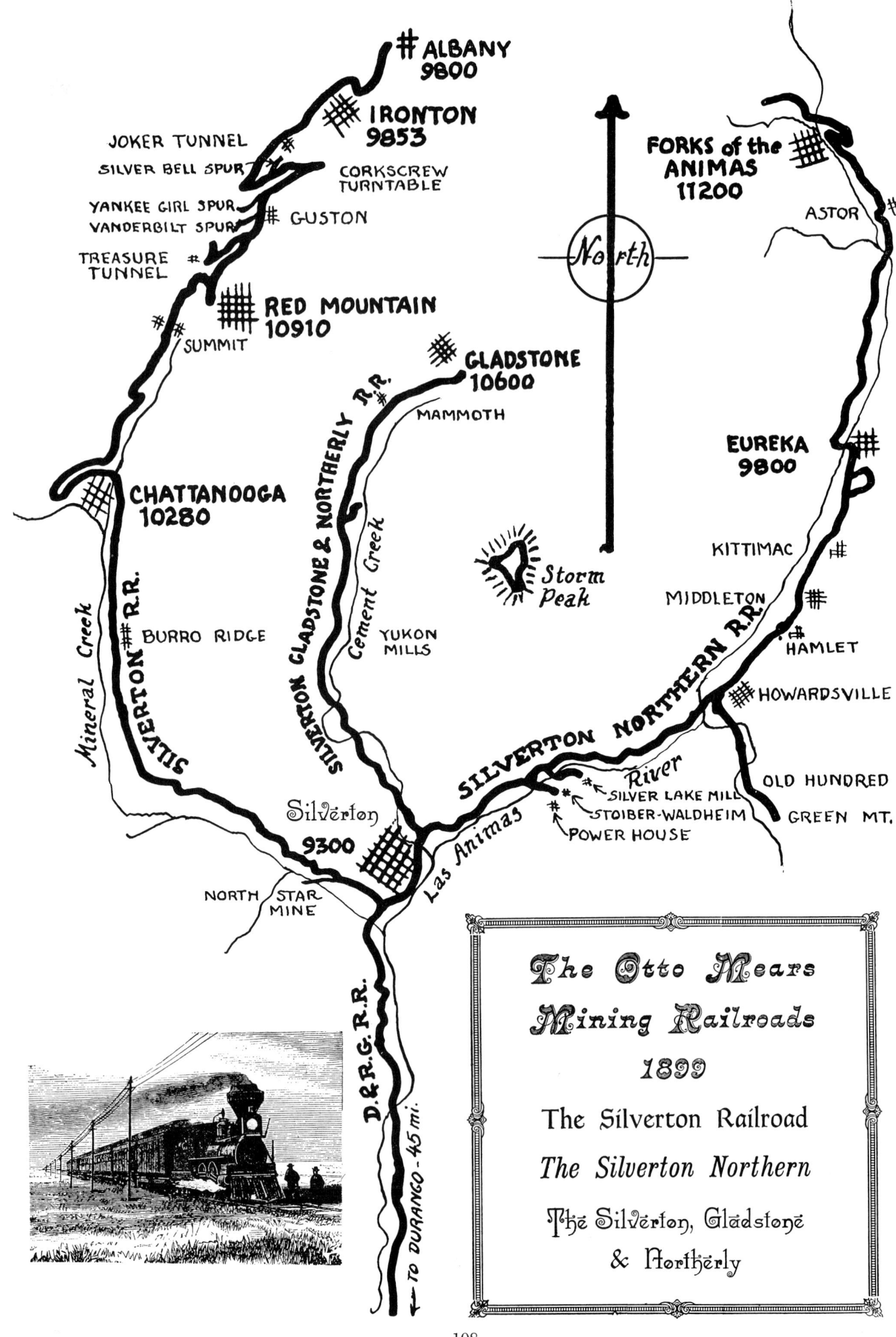

TWO PHOTOS: WESTERN COLLECTION

Like the more celebrated Galloping Geese of the Rio Grande Southern, this truly jaunty home-made rail car mounted on a Cadillac chassis was used in passenger service in the twenties on the run between Silverton and Eureka over the three-foot rails of the Silverton Northern Railroad. It was patterned on the more professionally devised and far more capacious Galloping Geese. In the below photograph, a Silverton, Gladstone & Northerly train drawn by the engine *Gold King* poses for its portrait at Gladstone. The map on the page opposite depicts the Mears mining railroads in the Uncompaghres as they converged upon the Rio Grande connection at Silverton.

R. W. RICHARDSON COLLECTION

Some idea of the elegance and ambitions of the little Mears roads running out of Silverton may be gained from the mahogany-finished Combine No. 2, outshopped by an Eastern car-builder for the Silverton, Gladstone & Northerly shortly after the turn of the century. AT LEFT: the wood burner No. 32 of the same line is shown during construction days a few miles out of Silverton, while at the bottom of the page, the straight stack and spoked wheels of the Silverton Northern's No. 3 have about them a mainline dimension and elegance that characterized the properties of the Pathfinder when he turned his hand to railroading in the towering Uncompahgres.

WESTERN COLLECTION

RICHARD KINDIG COLLECTION

The Silverton Railroad's geared locomotive *Ironton* (ABOVE) was reportedly traded to the Rio Grande Southern for two ordinary road engines. In the center is the Silverton's No. 34 as it was taken from the Silverton roundhouse in 1942, en route, as a wartime emergency measure, to the White Pass & Yukon in Alaska, while at the bottom is another view of Red Mountain and its mines in their greatest period of bonanza when the Silverton Railroad that served them was also operating in clover. The National Belle Mine shows on the hillslope, while in the gulch below, the Silverton's No. 100 appears posed on the spur track leading to the mine dumps.

RICHARD KINDIG COLLECTION

Wine List

SILVERTON NORTHERN RAILROAD CO.

Car: Animas Forks

	Dolls	Cts

LIQUORS

Private Stock Whiskey	per drink	$ .20
Greenbrier Bourbon Whiskey	per drink	.20
Scotch Whiskey	per drink	.20
Holland Gin	per drink	.20
Burke's Ale	per pint	.40
Burke's Stout	per pint	.40
Benedictine	per drink	.25
Green Chartreuse	per drink	.25

WATERS

Manitou Water	per quart	$ .35
Ginger Ale	per quart	.50
Red Raven Splits	per half pint	.20

WINES

Mumm's Extra Dry	per pint	$2.50
White Seal Champagne	per pint	2.50
Chateau Blanc Wine	per pint	.75
LaRose Wine	per pint	1.25
Grave's Wine	per pint	.75
Imported Sherry	per quart	2.50
Imported Port	per quart	2.50
Saarbuch Steinwein Wine	per pint	1.25
Liebfraumilch Wine	per pint	1.50
Sparkling Burgundy	per pint	1.50
California Port	per pint	1.25

Cigars and Cigarettes . . . .

Total

The wonder and glory of Otto Mears's narrow gauge short lines out of Silverton was the Pullman car *Animas Forks*, which was purchased from the Rio Grande Railroad and rebuilt at the Silverton shops as a combination restaurant and sleeping car as depicted below. An elaborate wine card printed in two colors (PAGE OPPOSITE) and an equally ornate menu listing Russian caviar, mock turtle soup, Hamburg grapes and other exotic delicacies made the little club car, as Mears intended, the talk of the San Juan, and its fame spread throughout the entire West to the greater profit and promotion of the Silverton Northern and its allied railroads. Not even the far-flung Denver & Rio Grande Western, whose narrow gauge dining cars provided the best of everything when the best was very good indeed, possessed greater refinement than the wine closet of the *Animas Forks* (LEFT) with its resources of vintage champagnes, rare Rhine wines and potent spirits. Contemporaries commented that Otto Mears missed no bets in achieving favorable celebrity for his properties.

AUTHORS' COLLECTION   ROBERT RICHARDS

The Silverton Railroad
The Silverton Northern
Club Car **Animas Forks**

WESTERN COLLECTION

Nothing in the operation of the Silverton Railroad, not even its dining car nor its phenomenal profits in the early years, was more fascinating to engineers and collectors of railroad curiosa than its turntable at Corkscrew Gulch roofed over as a protection against the heavy snows of winter. The photographs on this and the page opposite indicate the desolate mountain background against which the rich and swaggering little carrier operated its diminutive trains.

WESTERN COLLECTION

A curiosity in Colorado folklore holds that the covered turntable at Corkscrew Gulch was, sometime subsequent to its construction in 1888, knocked down and set up again near Forks of Animas on the Silverton Northern. Here it is shown from below track level at Corkscrew Gulch in a companion photograph to that on the page opposite.

RICHARD KINDIG

That the story of the turntable's removal is a canard is evidenced by this photograph taken by Richard Kindig in September, 1951, showing the turntable base still intact at Corkscrew Gulch with a pine tree growing through its ties as testimony of its permanence at the site. In the photo are E. J. Haley and M. C. Poor, the latter the dedicated historian of the South Park.

115

Otto Mears's genius for publicity and promotion was in inverse proportion to the size of the properties concerned, and the first silver passes were conceived to advertise a narrow gauge railroad whose aggregate trackage of mainline and branches was less than twenty miles. That his expansive gestures of publicization and hospitality paid off would seem, at this remove, undeniable. Mears's name was good on notes in the banks not only of Durango and Denver but in far-off New York, where it was favorably known to the titans of finance who assembled at the bar of the Windsor Hotel and under the bear and bull at the Waldorf Astoria. The passes in precious metals which Mears carried with him when he completed the Rio Grande Southern are today a rare item of Colorado memorabilia and a special field of information for informed railroad historians. One of the handful of known Mears passes in buckskin shown at the top of this page is the property of the authors of this book, to whom it was presented by A. M. Camp, senior banker and grand old man of the San Juan region, "as a small recognition for your services to the San Juan." The pass was originally issued to A. P. Camp, Mr. Camp's father and one of the pioneers of Southwestern Colorado, but the ink in which his name and that of Mears himself was engrossed has long since faded without trace from the aging leather.

COLLECTION OF ROBERT RICHARDSON

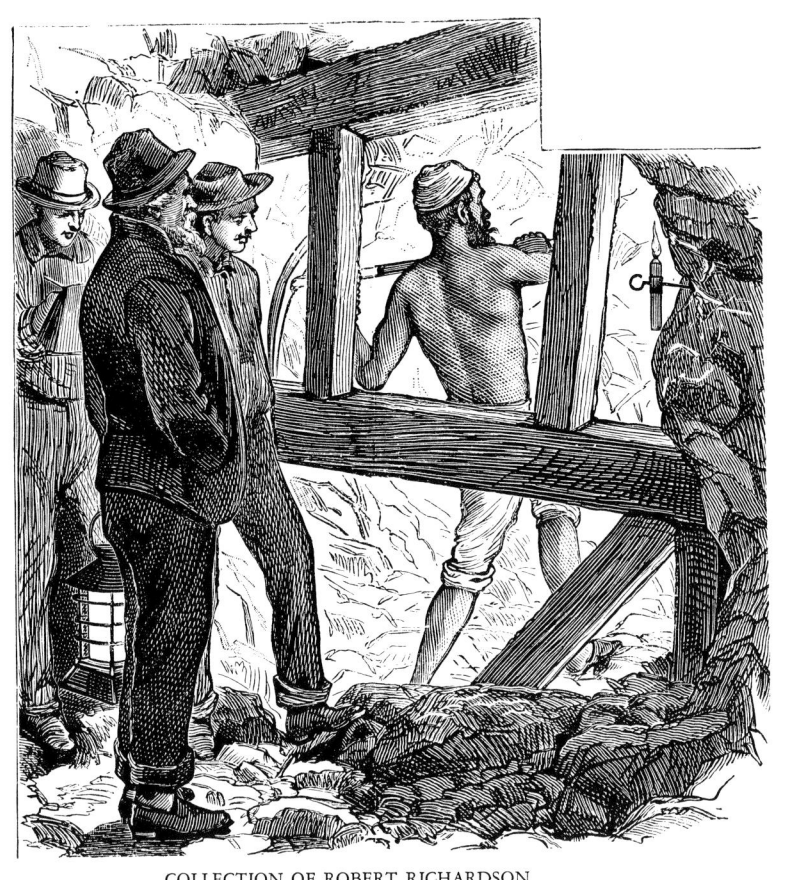

Until comparatively recent years, much speculation as to the cost and other details of the Mears passes was current in Colorado historical circles, but in 1952, Robert Richardson of Alamosa discovered in the company's files at Ridgway the invoice reproduced here showing that one lot of silver passes was manufactured for the Pathfinder by a Santa Fe silversmith at a cost of four dollars each. To heighten their associational value, Mears himself watched the mining of the ore at the Yankee Girl at Red Mountain (LEFT) and was able to tell recipients of his gifts that he had supervised the preparation of the passes from the moment their ore was recovered from the very womb of geologic time.

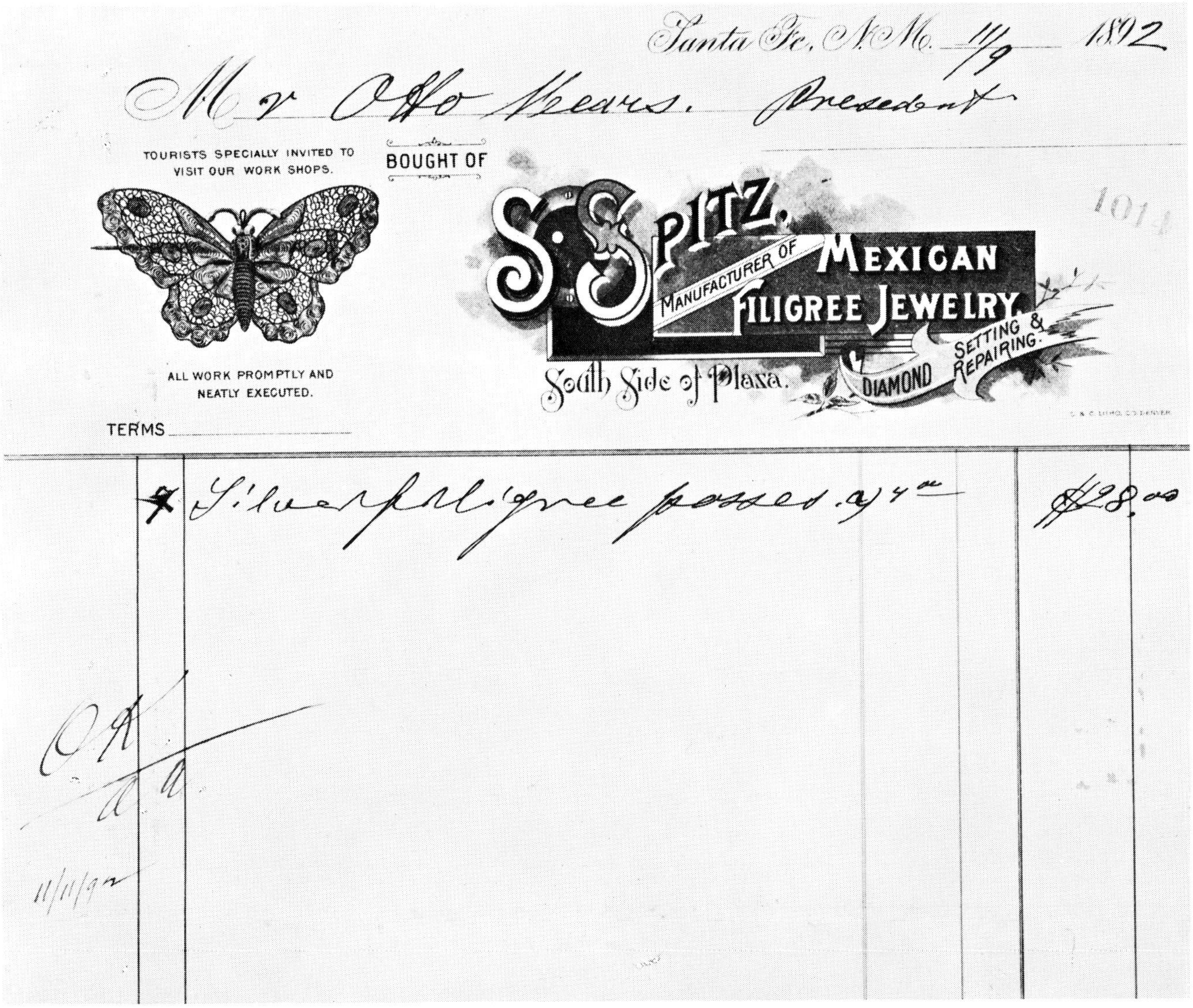

Santa Fe, N.M. 11/9 1892

Mr Otto Mears. President

TOURISTS SPECIALLY INVITED TO VISIT OUR WORK SHOPS.

BOUGHT OF

1014

S. SPITZ, MANUFACTURER OF MEXICAN FILIGREE JEWELRY

South Side of Plaza.

DIAMOND SETTING & REPAIRING.

ALL WORK PROMPTLY AND NEATLY EXECUTED.

TERMS

7	Silver filigree passes @ 4.00	$28.00

OK

A A

11/11/92

JACK THODE COLLECTION

WESTERN COLLECTION

Trip Around the Circle

Through Realms of Gold and Silver,

VIA

Between Silverton and all points in the famous

Red Mountain Country

Connects with the Denver and Rio Grande R. R. at Silverton and Ouray, and completes the famous trip

"AROUND ✦ THE ✦ CIRCLE"

Over Denver and Rio Grande Railroad, acknowledged to be the most magnificent mountain trip in the known world, including daylight ride of six miles in CONCORD COACHES through the Uncompahgre Canon which is unequalled in its grandeur and adds greatly to the pleasure of this delightful journey.

OTTO MEARS,
President, DENVER.

MOSES LIVERMAN,
Gen. Superintendent,
SILVERTON.

S. K. HOOPER,
Gen. Pass. Agt.,
DENVER.

The fearful winters in the Uncompaghre altitudes saw frequent tragedies in the mining camps, when avalanches swept down from the peaks and canyon trails were obliterated for months on end. In the drawing (BELOW) from the pages of *The Police News* published in far-off Boston is depicted a miner's cabin on Copper Creek not many miles from Ironton, where a springtime rescue party discovered the body of a miner who had perished many weeks before. In his pockets was a fortune in currency which had proved useless to purchase the necessities of life when he was cut off from the outer world. At the left is one of Otto Mears's advertisements for the Silverton Railroad when it had been completed to the Red Mountain country and before the Rio Grande Southern had been built. The "Narrow Gauge Circle" then went from Durango to Silverton on the D&RGW, thence to Red Mountain on the Silverton Railroad, and the gap to Ouray was spanned, as it was always destined to be, by stage road. On the page opposite, some idea of the four per cent grades at Chattanooga may be gained from the Jackson photograph (BELOW) while (ABOVE) on a rainy day long ago the D&RGW's narrow gauge No. 22 and the Silverton's No. 100 pose at two levels on the selfsame loop with Mears himself barely discernible in a raincoat by the lower engine.

RICHARD KINDIG COLLECTION

JOHN W. MAXWELL

The Ouray stub of the D&RGW was possessed of a special hold on the imagination of railroad fanciers by reason of the primal simplicities of servicing—stub switches, a manually operated turntable, and simple water connection—shown above against the mountainside that makes Ouray a formidable cul-de-sac in the landscape. Otto Mears would dearly have loved to achieve Ouray's splendid Beaumont Hotel (PAGE OPPOSITE) via his Silverton Railroad, but the valley was pervious only from the north and by the Rio Grande which, to be sure, connected with Mears's Rio Grande Southern at Ridgway. In the lower frames, No. 318 with a short consist of mixed freight rolls into Ouray over a low trestle for a smoky profile of narrow gauge railroading in the grand manner.

WESTERN COLLECTION

Almost as beguiling as the little railroads that served them was a generation of Colorado hotels to which pilgrims resorted when they stepped down from the three-foot Palace cars. The lordly Windsor and palatial Brown in Denver were matched by the Antlers at Colorado Springs, the Clarendon and Vendome in Leadville, the Teller House at Central City, Hotel de Paris at Georgetown, the Grand at Silverton and La Veta at Gunnison which were and in some cases still are notable properties in the spacious legend of the Rockies. At Ouray the Beaumont was one of this ornate tradition and stands to this day as a monument to the uninhibited tastes and architecture of the golden years.

RICHARD KINDIG

OTTO PERRY

Denver, South Park & Pacific

It is difficult in the long lexicon of American regional sentiment to discover a vanished institution that still lays as compulsive a hold on the imagination of thousands who never saw it as the narrow gauge Denver, South Park & Pacific Railroad. True, it is not widely celebrated outside the boundaries of Colorado, but in the Shining Mountains of recollected things it is a legend comparable to the Windsor Hotel in its glory, Buffalo Bill's thirst, or the gestures of remembered splendor of Spencer Penrose. Only the Rio Grande Southern is its peer as a wistful souvenir of *temps jadis*.

Certainly no short line railroad ever to be included in the *Official Guide*, not even the Virginia & Truckee or the East Tennessee & Western North Carolina, known to the Grandfather Mountain country as "Tweetsie," boasted such regional devotion. No railroad in the history of the flanged wheel, not even the lordly Pennsylvania or the ineffable Union Pacific, can boast the bibliography owned by the South Park. Its story has been engrossed for perpetuity in a book by M. C. Poor of 500 quarto pages, embracing well over half-a-million words of letterpress together with half-tones, maps, graphs, statistical tables, and an index and other critical apparatus that would do credit to the mythology of the Holy Grail or the Arthurian

Legend. This imposing artifact issued in an edition of 1,000 by the members of the Rocky Mountain Railroad Club as devotional reading for The Faithful was impressively subscribed at a substantial price before publication and today commands a sum among collectors only limited by the purse of the purchaser.

No cathedral of Gothic antiquity, or medieval veneration can boast a more tangible tribute to invincible piety. It is even said that The Faithful, wherever they may be, turn their faces daily toward Boreas Pass and Alpine Tunnel, but this may well be apocryphal.

The ownership, control, and administration of the affairs of the South Park is a record of such involved change and exchange of managements as to be confusing to the professional railroad historian and almost meaningless to the amateur or mere admirer of its folkways and tangible evidences.

It started in business, in the fall of 1872, as the Denver, South Park & Pacific Railroad and retained this style and title until 1889, during which period its control passed successively to Jay Gould's complex of railroad properties in 1880 and a year later to the Union Pacific. In 1890, its operating title was changed to the Denver, Leadville & Gunnison Railway whose stock was held and management vested in the corporate entity of the Union Pacific, Denver & Gulf Railway, and in 1898, the entire setup was acquired by the Colorado & Southern which in turn passed, in 1908, into the hands of the Chicago, Burlington & Quincy Railroad. Thus, for the last years of its operating lifetime, it bore the insigne of the Colorado & Southern under the controlling ownership of the Burlington.

Throughout all these phases of its useful and often exciting lifetime, it was known to travelers and to Coloradans merely as the South Park and that title will suffice here.

In 1879, the Union Pacific had, in addition to the South Park, acquired ownership of the Colorado Central, reaching variously to Golden, Black Hawk, Central City, and by the South Fork of Clear Creek to Idaho Springs and Georgetown. In 1890, the narrow gauge system was merged in the over-all Union Pacific, Denver & Gulf Railway which, in the same year, acquired its extension, the Georgetown, Breckenridge & Leadville road, scene of the celebrated Georgetown Loop, so that in the final phase of their operations, the South Park and the Colorado Central were one and the same property under the banner of the Colorado & Southern. Even in the chronicle of these remote and microscopic narrow gauge carriers might be discerned the pattern of consolidation and unification which in a few years was to characterize the far greater facade of railroading along the mainlines of the entire United States.

Bugles were blowing behind the Ramparts of the Shining Mountains when Denver businessmen in satin-faced frock coats and beautifully striped cashmere trousers first started dreaming of the railroad that was to become the South Park. The notes were high and silvery, like French horns, and elusive, but they persisted and, shortly, they were augmented by fiddle music playing "Clementine" and the quicksteps of the old frontier that still shiver the souls of men when they are played today. By the time the cars and engines were running through Platte Canyon, it was a mighty symphony thundering the golden crescendos of wealth, tangible in gold and silver, that have always been closer to the American heart than other more spiritual fulfillments.

At the time it started business as a common carrier out of Denver, the South Park partook of the simple geographic definition which was to characterize Colorado railroading for two full decades and vestigial traces of which survive to this day in the fugitive fragments of the Denver & Rio Grande Western that still operate to three-foot gauge. All railroads built or building into Colorado, or that were to be constructed in years to come east of the Rocky Mountains, were of standard gauge. Until the commencement of the ill-fated Colorado Midland, every foot of track laid west of the Ramparts was narrow gauge. A ruled line from Cheyenne through Denver City, Colorado Springs, and Pueblo to Trinidad would neatly have set off the one philosophy of railroad construction from the other. General William Jackson Palmer was the archprophet of narrow gauge, and neither the standard tracks of Union Pacific to the north nor of the impending Santa Fe to the south were to change his thinking for two full decades. Like the Denver & Rio Grande, the South Park was prenatally conditioned to be three feet wide and no more.

Moving agent in the original organization and projection of the Denver, South Park & Pacific was Colorado's Governor John Evans, familiarly known as "Napoleon" Evans because of the imperial dimensions of his ambitions and his genius for organization. Its articles of association were made a matter of record in June, 1873, and its objective as stated therein was the construction of a narrow gauge steam railroad out of Denver to Morrison, and also up South Platte Canyon "across the Valley of the Arkansas River and through the Poncha Pass and across the San Luis Valley to or near the town of Del Norte and thence by the most feasible route to the San Juan mining districts in South Western Colorado—to be extended thence to the Pacific Ocean."

No railroad promoters of the period in their right minds but included a Pacific terminal in their corporate title and the South Park was no exception. It never, of course, achieved the Pacific and it never penetrated the San Juan mining region, but it did prosper to become the largest narrow gauge system wholly contained within the boundaries of Colorado. With 339 miles of mainline and branches, it topped the continental divide twice at altitudes in excess of 11,000 feet, and its operations and properties became a durable element of the Colorado legend.

The first rails laid on the South Park's right of way through what is now suburban Denver but was then the open Colorado countryside were of iron and weighed but thirty pounds to the yard. Its graders quite literally shovelled their few perfunctory yards of earth—there was no grade in the formal sense—around large boulders and substantial trees rather than expend the time and powder to blast a straight passage through. Cy Warman, the railroad poet and himself a one-time fireman on the narrow gauge, later remarked that the road's "little locomotives could curve on the brim of a sombrero." As a matter of fact, the longest single tangent on the entire railroad was 7.84 miles on the Fairplay branch.

In 1878 the South Park was still very much a railroad from nowhere to nowhere making its way precariously up Platte Canyon, when the resounding tidings of California Gulch turned the eyes of the world toward Leadville. Leadville overnight provided incentive, purpose, and direction for the construction of two railroads, neither of which was until then entirely sure where it was going. General Palmer's Denver & Rio Grande and Governor Evans's South Park were the logical contenders in the race for the rich Leadville traffic in everything from carbonate ores and pick handles to prefabricated bagnios and three-card monte throwers, and Governor Evans, either prudently or by merest chance, had included in the articles of the South Park a branch to the headwaters of the Arkansas in Lake County. The South Park's advantage lay in a route of only 170 miles between Denver and Leadville to the Rio Grande's 280-mile line up the Arkansas Valley via Pueblo, but

General Palmer's carrier had the advantage in already being big business with money and professional know-how at its disposal.

The ensuing race was one of the epics of the golden age of railroad construction and rivalry in the Old West. Sensing a means to secure through interchange the traffic that had been denied it when the route up the Arkansas went to General Palmer, the Atchison, Topeka & Santa Fe entered the picture with an attempted alliance with the South Park, a move which was shortly countered by Jay Gould, who bought a half-interest in the Rio Grande while at the same time throwing the long shadow of Gould power over the South Park itself.

By now the South Park had achieved an end of track at Kenosha, where the old Mosquito Pass wagon road was doing business of bonanza proportions as the shortest and most direct connection with Leadville. Mining machinery and whisky, madames, Cousin Jack hard-rock men, beef and beer, all the necessities of an up-and-coming camp went in, and ore and bullion for the smelters at Denver made a profit on the return trip as well. M. C. Poor, official historian of the South Park, remarked that it was definitely an act of Providence that the arrival of the narrow gauge in South Park should coincide so precisely with the emergence of Leadville as the carbonate capital of the West.

By the year 1880, when the South Park and the Rio Grande arrived in Buena Vista on the Arkansas together, Gould had acquired a controlling interest in Governor Evans's road and the narrow gauge was enjoying an era of profitable operation even in its incompleted state. Gould foresaw no profit to either of the companies in which he was interested if rivalry was carried to the extreme of building two separate railroads from Buena Vista into their common goal of Leadville, and under his pressure and orders, the South Park and the Rio Grande shared trackage rights up the Arkansas and into the booming carbonate capital. This was the first of the South Park's two routes to Leadville, the other being the so-called "High Line" from Como to Breckenridge, Kokomo and Climax, which was achieved after Gould had sold his control of the South Park to the Union Pacific and was a venture inspired and organized out of Omaha rather than Denver.

The move was dictated primarily by bad feeling over the sharing of Leadville traffic between the South Park and the Rio Grande over the joint trackage to Buena Vista and entailed a long jog to the north out of Como, the crossing of the continental divide at Boreas Pass, and the slightly longer leg of a triangle down the west slope of the Range into Breckenridge and Dickey and then up Tenmile Canyon to Climax. The route was still twenty-one miles shorter than the Buena Vista entry.

The Leadville High Line was commenced with great energy on the part of the Union Pacific in August, 1883, and was completed, despite every effort and legal devising of the Rio Grande to prevent it, into Leadville by February of the following year. Even so, the South Park was not to taste the fruits of its labor immediately. An uncommonly formidable winter set in; the little tracks and narrow right of way at Boreas and Climax were impassable and completely impervious to plows, and in order to retain an entry to Leadville, the Union Pacific was in the humiliating position of having to ask General Palmer's road to allow it to extend the joint trackage agreement into the spring. When, finally, in the summer of 1884, regular passenger and freight traffic was scheduled between the South Park's two terminals, it required 151 miles of track making ninety-seven complete circles and climbing three major mountain ranges to cover an airline distance of only seventy-seven miles.

All the Rocky Mountain region hailed the entrance of the three-foot carrier into Leadville. The economy of the state as a whole was so closely bound to the mining of precious metals that the successful commerce of Leadville was reflected throughout the entire state and on July 4, 1880, *The Rocky Mountain News* ran a full-dress account of the South Park's progress and achievements under the following bank of headlines. The "45 miles of Rail" refers not to any portion of the operating track, but to a reserve of "steel rail to be used in repairing the track and keeping it as near perfection as it now is."

The South Park

Pioneer Railroad to the Carbonate Camp

ELEGANT COACHES

What The Company Has Done

For Denver

45 Miles of Rail

Daily passenger service with a $12.50 fare was at once established between the South Park's two terminals on a schedule which required from 8:45 in the morning to 6:15 in the evening. An engine house with eight stalls for its iron ponies was built at the Leadville end, and the conventional "new and elegant passenger depot" was contemplated at Denver. The South Park at once achieved a reputation of being a strictly cash, full-fare carrier, for, and contrary to the almost universal practice elsewhere in Colorado, passes were kept at an irreducible minimum.

From the outset, Colorado was filled with admiration for its railroads in general and their locomotives in particular. Far away in England, the steamcars were being given a rough time by esthetes and philosophers, in particular by John Ruskin, whose special revulsion and detestation were reserved for the smoking locomotives and their trailing train brigades which were raising hell with the tranquillity of the English countryside. Ruskin laid a swinging long curse on railroad progress. It filled the landscape with unsuitable persons and the engines themselves were simply terrible. If only they might be possessed of some esthetic charm, some diminution of their fearful utilitarian facade, it wouldn't be so bad! Engines might be disguised, Ruskin suggested, to resemble the properties of classic mythology, say wyverns or dragons, their smoke spouting through the distended nostrils of heraldic fancy with beating wings instead of merely functional side rods and valve gear.

Colorado in the seventies took a less austere view of things and openly delighted in the gay little engines that the South Park ordered from Dawson & Bailey, the Brooks Locomotive Works, or the erecting shops of William Mason in far-off

Taunton, Massachusetts. Early delegations of railroad buffs passed judgment on the diminutive valve gear and gleaming drivers of the *Fairplay* and *Oro City* as they went on their lawful occasions to Morrison and Bear Creek Junction and a few years later were rapturous over the gold scrollwork and fine-lining of such marvels of compacted power as the *Breckenridge* and *Twin Lakes*. The first primeval passenger equipment, outshopped by Hallack Brothers in Denver, was not as magnificently upholstered as some, but was generally regarded as satisfactory.

While these heady doings were toward the direction and vicinity of Leadville, the South Park was simultaneously prosecuting another major project of the moment, the completion of a line to Gunnison, which was also in the throes of a mining boom to rival that of Leadville itself in magnitude and intensity. Silver had been found at Gunnison as early as 1870, but the hostility of the Utes had discouraged prospectors. A Dr. Sylvester Richardson had started a socialist agricultural colony something like that at Greeley on the edge of the Great Plains and it had been a resounding failure. Now, in 1879, silver in truly important quantities had been uncovered at nearby Crested Butte and Gunnison had emerged as another bonanza that clamored for a railroad to serve its municipal needs.

The Denver newspapers carried insertions asking for workmen to lay track out of Buena Vista, and specially urgent was the appeal for experienced tunnel and hard-rock miners to help dig a gigantic tunnel at Alpine.

One of the great legends of the South Park was the Alpine Tunnel.

The Alpine bore was constructed about halfway between Buena Vista and Gunnison on the Gunnison line to penetrate the backbone of the Saguache range at the continental divide at an altitude of almost 12,000 feet, where winter blizzards raged, and rage to this day with an almost unimaginable fury. It was planned as a single track tunnel 1,800 feet long, blasted largely through solid granite, but when construction was actually under way, it was discovered that fewer than 100 feet of the entire length was of self-supporting solid rock formation. The remainder was through decomposed granite frequently penetrated by subterranean streams and the contractors were required to arch and timber almost the entire length with twelve by twelves of California redwood to the extent of 1,500,000 feet of this expensive wood costing upwards of $100 a thousand.

At the high altitude, which inhibited the exertions of laborers accustomed to denser atmospheres, and in extremities of cold with the primitive earth-moving tools of the time, Alpine Tunnel was an engineering undertaking of formidable proportions.

A snowshed 150 feet long was built at the east portal and 650 feet of protective wooden tunnel at the west portal, access to each of which was through heavy timber doors which excluded the elements and had to be opened manually for the passage of all trains in winter. Construction was slow and hazardous. Blizzards howled around the approaches to the bore with such fury that they could only be reached from the construction camps at either end by human chains. Despite the then high salary of $3.00 a day for tunnel workers, the labor turnover was enormous and once, when an Italian was hanged at Gunnison for murder, an entire shift of Italian hard-rock men walked off in protest. There was the accustomed loss of life from delayed blasts, defective powder work, and rock slides. A single premature dynamite blast killed forty-eight workers. One firm of contractors, which had expended an initial $50,000 for supplies alone and built a $25,000 wagon road from Pitkin to the portal, went bankrupt, and a second contracting firm took up the

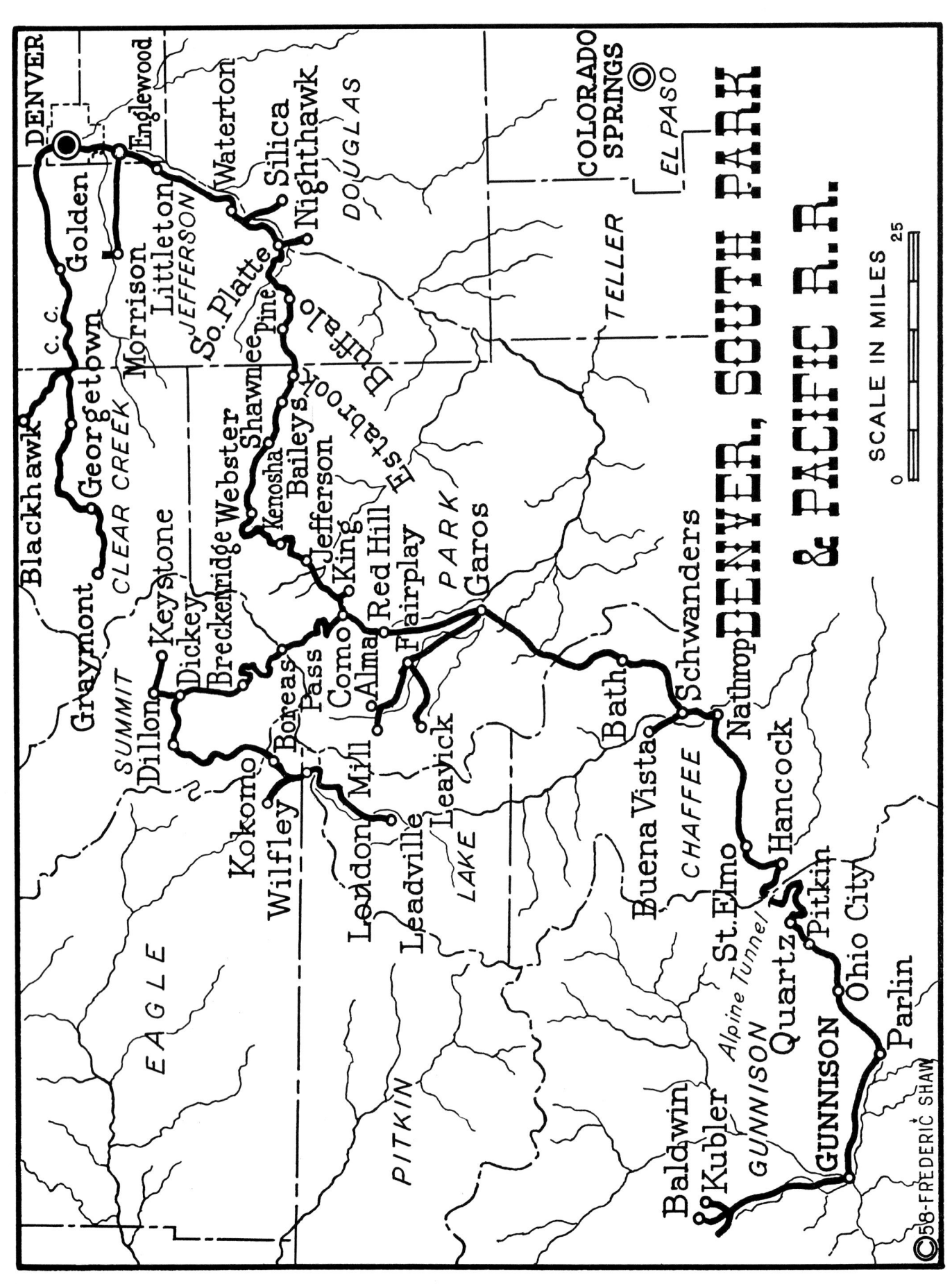

challenge and put 1,000 men to work on a twenty-four-hour-a-day schedule throughout the year 1880.

Engineering journals all over the world and, of course, the Colorado newspapers followed the progress of the undertaking with detailed reports until, in July of 1881, the headings of the tunnel met and the South Park was free to lay track into Gunnison.

From the two portals, the tracks worked on grades averaging one per cent toward an apex where a great storm lantern with red glass was kept burning from one year to another to let engineers know when to stop working steam. At Alpine Tunnel station, a vast stone engine house was erected, together with coal bins, water tanks, and other resources for fueling locomotives at the top of their long climb. There was a bunkhouse, permanent quarters for a station agent, telegrapher, and watchman who patrolled the entire length of the tunnel itself at frequent intervals, and a company dining room presided over by a mammoth female whose buttercakes and antelope steaks were famous all over the South Park. Train crews who got snowed in at Alpine counted themselves in luck.

The first train to run through Alpine Tunnel to Pitkin was a special loaded with dignitaries and also, as it turned out, catastrophe. Twenty South Park officials and their wives, including the Union Pacific's wealthy Sydney Dillon, were aboard a Pullman sleeper behind engine No. 11, the *Ouray*, when the train ran wild and the coupling behind the locomotive broke at Midway tank. The passengers leaped to safety and the South Park's chief engineer, L. H. Eicholtz, broke an arm and a leg to boot.

The first regular train to arrive on operating schedule was in better luck. Aboard the four coaches and head end revenue cars were the U.S. Mail, an agent of the Pacific Express Company, and Williams' Theatrical Troupe with a production of repertory including "East Lynne" and "Money", the latter a favored theme with all Coloradans of the time. There were speeches, the firing of giant powder, and four barrels of beer for the train crew.

Like other tunnels before and since where fatalities have been involved, Alpine in its operating lifetime acquired a sinister reputation known as "The Curse of Alpine," rehearsed in more detail elsewhere in this chapter. To this day the ruins of the once great and populous bore under the continental divide is supposed to be haunted by the ghost of Dad Martinis who died there at the controls of his engine, probably from an accumulation of carbon gas.

Another of the legends that cluster around the South Park thick as autmn leaves on Valambrosa is that of the circus train en route to Leadville one winter long ago, with the big tent, animals, and performers of Barnum & Bailey's Greatest Show on Earth. Somewhere on the grade north of Climax, steam failed the teapot locomotive assigned to the circus train and Leadville was in a fair way to be without a circus that night. At this impasse, a circus executive remembered the elephants. The mahouts were routed out of the sleeping car, the elephants detrained on the right of way, and two of the great beasts put their heads against the rear car to push the train over the hump. The event became an imperishable part of Colorado folklore.

Still another South Park legend was the fishermen's trains which did a specially prosperous business in the nineties running between Denver and Grant and setting out sportsmen along South Platte Canyon at points they might designate to the conductor. The fish trains left Denver late in the afternoon, and many Izaak

Waltons had cabins or lean-tos along the river where they spent the night. In the morning, all they had to do to get back to town was to step up to the right of way and wave a handkerchief at the engineer. Sometimes there were two and three sections to the fish trains on Saturdays and Sundays in summertime.

The South Park reached Gunnison September 1, 1882, and the ensuing celebration left its first citizens palsied and twitching for days to come. A row of beer kegs was set up beside the track and at nine o'clock, the appropriately named Hon. Alexander Gullett ascended a card table which served as a speaker's stand and urged the multitude to fall to. Hose Company No. 2, in full dress uniform, kept comparative order as speaker followed speaker, each in turn exploring the seemingly limitless vistas of prosperity opened by the coming of the wonderful steamcars. Last speaker of all and infinitely the most popular was Mayor Moses, who declaimed: "Boys, I'm not much of an orator but if you will follow me to the Switch Key saloon, I will set them up for everybody."

Gunnison and its mines did indeed boom for several years after the coming of the South Park and was also the division point on the Rio Grande's Marshall Pass mainline en route to Utah. In 1884, things were so brisk that Gunnison achieved in La Veta Hotel what was easily the most stupefying hostelry on the Western Slope, a four-story structure of seemingly limitless apartments, whose owner hit on the promotional scheme of serving free meals to guests on days when the sun failed to shine on fortunate Gunnison. In twenty-five years, La Veta was only called on to pony up with the steaks and chops seventeen times.

The Clear Creek line, which eventually achieved Black Hawk and Central City on its northern branch and Georgetown on its southern, was an afterthought with the objective of connecting the Gilpin mines to the standard gauge Colorado Central Railroad between Denver and Golden. The original survey up Clear Creek had been made by Captain Edward L. Berthoud, whose memory is perpetuated to this day in Berthoud Pass, and it was first expected that the road would naturally, as an enlargement and connection of the Colorado Central, be standard gauge. But the prohibitive cost of standard construction up the tortuous canyon of the creek and the exemplary economy of General Palmer's Rio Grande caused the eventual adopting of the three-foot gauge which was to operate for seventy-odd years.

When the tracks on the North Fork of Clear Creek reached Black Hawk in 1872, they encountered a dead end which threatened to terminate the line at that point in the form of an enormous and costly stone stamp mill that had been built on the river bank in a moment of optimism by a group of New York capitalists who had subsequently gone broke even before machinery was installed. On one side, the mill was flanked by the river, on the other by the mountain, and there was no room in either direction for even a three-foot roadbed. The Colorado Central solved the problem by purchasing the mill structure for the proverbial song and running the tracks right through and out the other side on their way to Central City. It gave Black Hawk a railroad station of such metropolitan dimensions as to rival Denver, and the trains stopped under an imposing roof, no small consideration in the Colorado winters.

The year the Colorado Central reached Black Hawk saw the gala opening at neighboring Central City of the Teller House, destined to be one of the most celebrated caravansaries of the entire West and still in operation today, and it was hoped that the Teller's guests would soon be arriving aboard the steamcars to partake of its staggering menu and well-stocked bar. But the panic of 1873 put an end to railroad financing everywhere and not for five long years was the cheery tooting of the narrow gauge audible the length of Eureka Street. When the line was completed, however, the cuisine and other creature comforts of the Teller served as an incentive to tourists and others with business in the region in much the same manner that French Louis Du Puy's Hotel de Paris at Georgetown brought knowing travelers in aboard the South Fork branch.

Notables and celebrities by the score, including the inevitable President Grant and Horace Tabor, rode the narrow gauge to Central, and Gene Fowler, one of the Rocky Mountain region's foremost historians, has written his recollections of the run for the authors of this book.

"My most durable memory of the narrow gauges of my youth," says Fowler, "is of the ride on the Colorado & Southern to Georgetown near where my father went to live in the mountains as a hermit some months before my birth. Probably he had foreknowledge of what was coming to him in my person.

"In my first recollection of the Georgetown train the locomotives had a common straight stack and as they moved upgrade in summer through the dry scrub and timber would set fire to the brush. Many complaints from the singed squatters above Golden went unanswered until one day a shower of sparks from Old No. 60 or whatever set the Silver Mountain Mill on fire and an hour or so later kindled and burned the Roman Catholic Church at Georgetown. To singe the behinds of plain citizens was one thing and of scant importance, but when both industry and religion were incinerated the railroad moved in for a swift do-something-about-it. As I recall the C&S paid $20,000 damages to the smoldering parties concerned and the engines thereafter wore a bonnet that may well have been an inspiration for Lily Daché at a later date.

"Denver in those days was winter quarters for the confidence men of the country. Sometimes they delayed their departure in the spring so as to visit the mining towns up Georgetown way, aboard the cars of course, to fleece investors on their way to the mines. This infuriated the hucksters of mining shares who hated to see a dollar wasted on a shell game when it could have gone into their own pockets and they were always after the railroad to get it to warn the passengers against monte throwers and green-goods vendors. So far as I recall the railroad never did anything about it, but was itself interested in the technique of skin game practitioners such as Soapy Smith, who was a good customer.

"Minor con men, a sort of race of lower vertebrates of the fast pitch, masqueraded as news butchers and sold various wares up and down the trembling aisles: magazines, dime novels, candy, and smoked glasses of an uncommonly bilious blue shading. Thirty cents was a lot of money then and the glasses were no good for anything. The con artist butchers were occasionally able to persuade a green tourist to buy a pair of these glasses, saying that the rarified air and sun bouncing off the stone cliffs were apt to strike anyone stone-blind a week or so after exposure to sinister refraction of mountain light."

Two and one-tenth miles beyond the Georgetown terminal of the Clear Creek branch of the Colorado Central and 368 feet higher was Silver Plume, a mining town of some importance in the economy of the region which first to last produced $200,000,000 in gold, silver, copper, and lead within three decades. To achieve Silver Plume as its immediate objective and thence, in prospect up Sabine Gulch to the foot of Loveland Pass with the eventual destination of Breckenridge and Leadville, there was built the eight and one-half mile Georgetown, Breckenridge & Leadville Railroad which, for all its lofty purpose and ambition, ended at Graymont. The GB&L would have been just one more narrow gauge except for the dramatic presence of an engineering device that came to be known as the Georgetown Loop, through whose agency the distance by rail was extended from the two air-line miles between Georgetown and Silver Plume to four and a half miles with a gradient of 143 feet to the mile.

The tracks spiralled upward above the canyon of Clear Creek and passed over themselves by the celebrated high bridge, at the end of which trains were practically within seltzer squirt of Silver Plume depot with its handy Silver Plume Pavilion, an oasis maintained in the interest of tourist travel by the railroad. Under the management of the Union Pacific, into whose hands the GB&L, like the Colorado Central, eventually passed, the entire loop setup was widely exploited as a scenic attraction and as many as seven or eight special trains made the trip up Clear Creek from Denver daily in clement seasons, in addition to the two scheduled runs each way.

Twenty years after the construction of the Georgetown Loop, Silver Plume became the terminal of another narrow gauge railroad in the form of the Argentine Central, which was built to serve the Waldorf mining properties on the slope of Mt. McClellan. So abrupt were the grades of the Argentine line that Shay geared locomotives were the only adhesion motive power capable of operating over its wavy tangents and sky-high curves. Thus, Silver Plume and Georgetown became, for a brief time, the center of a complex of narrow gauges only rivalled in density of trackage and operations by Durango, Gunnison, and Leadville.

The years dealt impartially with mining in Colorado and with the narrow gauges and the decline of the one into terminal borrasca spelled the eventual end of the other. The last train out of Idaho Springs on the Clear Creek line of what was by now the Colorado & Southern rolled its string of high cars and gondolas past the venerable Argo Tunnel on May 4, 1941. Far away across the continental divide on the Leadville High Line, the war year of 1943 saw the final narrow gauge operation over the fourteen miles between Leadville and Climax which had already been tracked for broad gauge operation. The lights were going out one by one in Colorado's once populous mining towns and ancient rights of way were, mile by mile, being reclaimed by the wilderness or surfaced for the automobile car.

But the progress of decline and desolation knew one exception, and for a few years before it, too, joined the ghosts of heroic times the narrow gauge into Central City saw a startling revival in that metropolis of golden memories.

In 1932, a group of sentimental and magnificently solvent Denver citizens, among them Ann Evans, granddaughter of Napoleon Evans who had started the South Park, refurbished the handsome old Central City Opera House next to the equally historic Teller House in steep Eureka Street. The first of what was to be a spectacularly successful series of opera and play revivals starred Lillian Gish in *Camille*. The rest of the cast were Broadway players of the first magnitude; Robert Edmond Jones did the settings and an amiable moneybags named Delos Chappelle furnished the stage sets with veritable antiques at a reported cost of $75,000.

All the world, or so it seemed, came to Central City, some of them aboard Colorado & Southern business cars as far as Black Hawk, since the Central City depot had long been buried under the Chain-O-Mines tailing pond. Ann Evans was there, a frail but determined monument to the Colorado past; so was Spencer Penrose, who had built the Broadmoor Hotel at the Springs with Cripple Creek gold, Ethel Carlton, widow of Penrose's partner, Bert Carlton, who had for a time owned the Colorado Midland, Governor Ralph L. Carr and Boettchers, Reeds, and Hills and McFarlanes by the dozen. In another year, Central's by now dazzling first night was attended by the nation's greatest hostess of them all, Evalyn Walsh McLean, wearing the Hope diamond and the Star of the East, which had been financed so long ago from the Camp Bird at Ouray. Central recapitulated for the last time, in the years before the 1941 war, all of Colorado's glorious yesterdays.

Once again there were jewels, and evening dress, and champagne in the fine Victorian dining room of the Teller House, and names that made news in the great world on its register. And there were old timers, in claw-hammer tail coats, whose memories reached back to epic winters in Sagauche, and giant snowslides beyond Red Mountain, and ore trains with the hand brakes smoking down from Boreas Pass to Como—aye, to long-gone times in Fairplay and Leadville and Silver Plume, when all the world was young.

Now the old timers who revisited Eureka Street on those splendid nights are gone. So is the railroad gone with the men who built and rode it down the golden years, but it had a fine farewell in the knowledge that once again the opera at Central was lighted, that starched shirt-fronts were lining the bar at the Teller House, and that on the morning after first nights there were parties made up to see the Colorado sunrise from the dump of the Boston Mine. The stream of history that once had followed the narrow gauge flowed out of the past, and there was a continuity with yesterday.

So the South Park went to rest.

A rare old time photograph depicts South Park engines No. 199 and 196 double headed outside Alpine roundhouse, from the collection of Roy Graves of San Francisco, himself an old timer dating from the great days of steam in the Old West.

COLLECTION OF ROY D. GRAVES

The first stage in the construction of the South Park embraced the seventy-five miles to Kenosha Summit by way of the canyon of the South Platte as shown in this photograph taken somewhat later near Ferndale at milestone 38 out of Denver. In fifty miles of the river gorge, the right of way rose almost a mile higher than mile-high Denver and the entire ascent of the Platte was accomplished under conditions of extreme difficulty and often of danger. Where there was no shelf at all along the bank of the stream and cliffs rose sheer to a height of many hundred feet, workmen were lowered in slings from which they drilled holes in the face of the cliff to blast a narrow foothold with dynamite and nitroglycerine. Elsewhere, engineers labored waist-deep in an ice cold mountain torrent whose velocity of six miles an hour made drowning a hazard without the additional chore of placing and detonating charges of explosive. When, early in 1879, the track-laying gangs achieved Kenosha Pass at an altitude of 10,200 feet, many miles of construction had cost as much as $25,000, but the tangents of South Park beckoned and the company's treasury was in ample supply. Leadville and its fabulous traffic were a prize worthy of the effort.

WESTERN COLLECTION

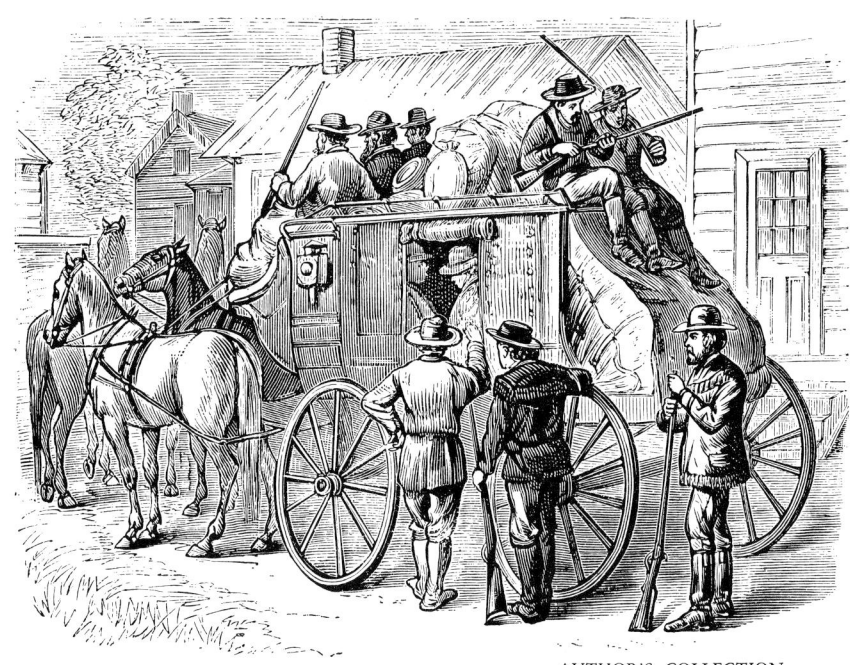

As the end of track of the South Park advanced toward Leadville, temporary stage stations set up by the teaming firm of Spotswood & McClellan moved west with the railroad, the distance of the staging run constantly diminishing as the track went down. The route was via Fairplay and Alma and over Mosquito Pass, where the elevation was a breathtaking 13,190 feet. When the South Park's end of track paused at Jefferson, the fare thence to Leadville was $17 in gold and the trip required the better part of two days. The advancing railhead and the ever-retreating staging route were part of the constant and ubiquitous pattern of the pioneer West.

AUTHOR'S COLLECTION

The indirect effects of the Leadville boom on the economy of the surrounding countryside were by no means negligible. Outfitting prospectors who required everything from Ames shovels and English self-cocking bulldog revolvers to hip boots, army blankets, and Franklin stoves became an important industry in Denver and along the way to the mines. Here a general merchandise store at Fairplay is shown dispensing what the well-dressed Cousin Jack will wear, at least until his estate justifies the frock coat, silk top hat, and gold Albert watch chain which will advertise to the world that he has struck it rich and is a man of consequence.

WESTERN COLLECTION

Although already notable for his financial subterfuge and stratagem, Jay Gould, when he arrived in Leadville via the cars of the South Park into which he was shortly to buy with disastrous effects, was a celebrity of the first chop and his words were reported as holy writ in the public prints. The year was 1880. Gould was accompanied by another New York moneybags in the person of Russell Sage, and together they journeyed over the rails of the South Park to Alpine Station, then the end of track, and made the balance of their journey by stage. "I am very much impressed with the South Park road and its earnings look good," said Gould, when the books showed that the profits of the incompleted narrow gauge for the year previous had been just under $1,000,000. Shortly thereafter Gould, who then controlled Union Pacific, and Governor John Evans of the South Park were horsetrading, and control of the carrier passed to U.P. headquarters at Omaha. BELOW is C&S No. 9 in the closing years of the South Park's operations passing Overland Park in Denver with train No. 71. This was the second No. 9, the first, the *Kenosha*, having been scrapped back in 1889.

CULVER SERVICE

OTTO PERRY

SARONY

Uncommonly conspicuous among the capitalists, burlesque queens, monte throwers and geologists who peopled the cars of the South Park was the arrival aboard the overnight sleeper from Denver in the eighties of Oscar Wilde, then on an American speaking tour for Major Pond's lecture bureau. Scheduled that evening to address a woman's society for improvement of the mind, Wilde was taken in hand to see the sights by a welcoming committee and eventually ended in the well-appointed bar of the Clarendon Hotel, whose lobby is depicted below, where it occurred to an irresponsible element among his hosts that it would be hilarious to get the celebrity of the moment in no fit shape to appear on the lecture platform in a few hours. Round followed round of potent libations, but Wilde appeared impervious to the strongest Bourbon. Members of the committee got their feet in cuspidors and started falling into potted palms, but Wilde was unruffled. Finally, at the appointed hour, the exponent of estheticism excused himself courteously from his glazed and shaken hosts and delivered his talk with perfect aplomb. Next day the conspirators had to admit to being hoist with their own petard and Wilde passed into Leadville legend as the hardest-headed drinker the town had ever encountered.

WESTERN COLLECTION

TWO PICTURES: WESTERN COLLECTION

Within six months of each other in 1880, two narrow gauge railroads, the Rio Grande and the South Park, arrived in Leadville and commenced competitive service that was to last as long as Leadville boomed to supply the greatest of all carbonate camps with the essentials of life ranging from bourbon whisky, roulette wheels and bedizened vaudeville performers to dynamite, rubber boots, heavy mining machinery and timbers for the winzes and crosscuts of the Little Johnny and Matchless. Dissolute beyond most, even in the tally of Colorado boom towns, Leadville provided an almost limitless market for all forms of vice and dissipation, running the gamut from the pretentious elegance of the bar at the Clarendon (LEFT), where the food was prepared by a chef from Delmonico's, to the notorious music halls on the order of the Little Casino, the Bon Ton, Red Light and Odeon, the last of which is depicted in a relaxed moment of culture on the page opposite. Everything necessary to a progressive mining camp—tinned oysters and boiled shirts for the nabobs, fascinators and fans for their ladies, lending libraries, crystal chandeliers and pick handles, and a personnel of gamblers, stockbrokers, claim jumpers, hard rock men, bunco steerers and evangelists—all came in on the steamcars. On this page is shown an early merchandise consist of the South Park on the Palisades at Alpine, and on the page opposite, a quadruple-header of the Colorado & Southern east of Waterton in 1937.

AUTHOR'S COLLECTION

OTTO PERRY

OTTO PERRY

ROBERT RICHARDS

The story of the circus train on the South Park which arrived in Leadville powered by the troupe's performing elephants when head-end motive power gave out has become an established item of Colorado folklore and mythology along with Soapy Smith, the eccentricities of Bonfils and Tammen and Packer, the man-eater who ate up all those Republicans. At the left, an artist has shown the stirring event in the wild embrace of a Colorado blizzard. At the top of the page, the Colorado & Southern's No. 69 and 70, the latter fitted to burn oil to save coaling on the run to Idaho Springs, pass through Waterton in 1941. The carloadings are silica and feldspar from South Platte, bound for the manufactories of Denver City.

Seen through the eye of William H. Jackson's omnipresent collodion plate camera from Kenosha Summit and the tracks of the Denver, South Park & Pacific, the South Park of the narrow gauge's corporate name stretches away in a splendid vista of sweeping distances toward Jefferson and, ultimately, Como.

WESTERN COLLECTION

The mines of Leadville, whose silver bricks (RIGHT) went down to Denver aboard the narrow gauge cars of the South Park and the Rio Grande in ever-increasing numbers, produced a generation of millionaires whose character ranged from the florid vulgarities of Horace Tabor to plodding, prudent, and acquisitive David Moffat who dreamed of a standard gauge railroad connection between Denver and the West that should one day by-pass the Rio Grande's long jog via Pueblo and Tennessee Pass. While other nabobs more or less quietly amassed wealth, it was Tabor whose profligate spending, financed by an incredible run of luck, became the symbol and archetype of Leadville success. His Matchless, Crysolite, Vulture, Maid of Erin and New Discovery mines stood the strain of frenzied finance which included traction companies that ran no streetcars, forests in Honduras that produced no mahogany, and, of course, diamonds, women, champagne, opera houses and fast horses. Leadville's strictly broad gauge financial operations rode to dizzying heights aboard the narrow gauge cars.

WESTERN COLLECTION

Of the Clarendon hotel, Leadville's most stylish hostlery, George Willison wrote: "The Clarendon Hotel on Harrison Avenue was likewise respectable, but with a difference. Less staid and sober than Tom Walsh's Grand Hotel, it shone with the well-dressed and bejeweled respectability of those who could afford the envious gossip of the vulgar. The lobby and bar were virtually the home of the Carbonate Kings. Here they discussed their business and personal affairs, conducted their negotiations and planned their coups. As they moved from bar to lobby and back again, they were trailed by business satellites, gentleman gamblers, brokers and promoters, sharpers of all kinds, and courtesans almost above reproach. The food at the Clarendon was excellent, prepared by Mr. A. LaPierce from Delmonico's, New York." Next door on Harrison Avenue was the passenger agency of the Denver & Rio Grande Railroad. Shortly after this picture was taken, Lt. Governor Tabor tired of the cuisine of Monsieur A. LaPierce, and gave his patronage to the Saddle Rock, also presided over by a graduate of Delmonico's, New York, a restaurant seemingly the source of all the chefs in Colorado. BELOW: No. 5 westbound on the South Park races upgrade with two cars into the snowsheds at Boreas Pass.

OTTO PERRY

No. 71, pictured in 1938 in Platte Canyon, drifts gently downgrade with smoke trailing lazily from a stack that came to be known throughout Colorado as a "beartrap."

RICHARD KINDIG

Harrison Avenue, Leadville, as it appeared in the false front and wooden sidewalk era, before the carbonate capital boasted paved streets, gas lamps, and other hallmarks of urban sophistication.

WESTERN COLLECTION

OTTO KUHLER

ROBERT RICHARDS

Como, where the rails diverged for Leadville and for Gunnison, in the mid-nineties was a scene of all-night activity as six regularly scheduled passenger trains converged upon and departed its yards and an uncounted number of freights pulled in for servicing. In the eighties, a decade before the scene depicted here by Otto Kuhler, the up-train from Denver had carried, in addition to head-end revenue and coaches, two sleepers, which presently departed in two different sections for Gunnison and Leadville respectively. Passengers who were awake joined the crew in taking precautions against the cold in the ample bar of the Pacific Hotel, but in 1896, the Pacific Hotel was spectacularly destroyed by fire and the through Pullmans had already been discontinued from regular service. Shown here is the new Como eating house, with No. 28, the *Denver*, and No. 63 panting gently in the Colorado night. Before the era of electric headlights, when extinguishing and rekindling a coal oil lamp was a real chore, engine crews, when they headed into a siding for a meet hung a shield, as shown below, over the lantern glass to avoid blinding the on-coming engineer.

From the Little Johnny Mine at Leadville (LEFT), the South Park rolled many hundreds of ore cars to the smelter, there to be translated into the tangible wealth that gratified the sometimes eccentric whims of Denver's "Unsinkable Mrs. Brown," heroine of the *Titanic*. Molly Brown's husband, "Leadville Johnny", only became a millionaire after he had inadvertently burned up his first fortune of $300,000 in banknotes in the stove. That very afternoon he located the Little Johnny, which produced uninterruptedly for many years. In 1936, a northbound extra on the South Park clattered through Sheridan Junction behind No. 9. There was a glory over the South Park even as the shadows gathered about the narrow gauge.

RICHARD KINDIG

Because of the number of lives that were sometimes lost in their construction, railroad tunnels often achieved a sinister reputation in regional folklore. None more so than the narrow gauge Denver, Leadville & Gunnison's Alpine Tunnel cutting directly across the continental divide at a level of 11,940 feet above the sea. Ute Indians were credited with having laid a comprehensive curse on the high country around Alpine Pass when white men destroyed the hunting there, and in 1884, thirteen lives were lost when a snowslide engulfed a train at Woodstock almost at the tunnel's portal. From 1888 to 1895, Alpine, the highest railroad pass on the continent, was closed to railroad traffic by reason of the heavy snows which rendered it inoperable for months at a time. The Curse of Alpine was an established Colorado legend by 1895, when it was decided to reopen the tunnel to traffic, and four members of the first train crew to enter it in seven years were killed by fumes from the engine working steam in its confined space. The engineer was found erect in his seat, his left hand on the air valve, his right on the reverse gear, his beard and working clothes neatly ordered. After that nobody doubted the existence of the Curse of Alpine. No trains have rolled through Alpine for many decades now and neighbors say it is haunted by the ghost of Dad Martinis carrying his spectral hands before him just as they rested on the controls of his locomotive at the end.

BELOW: the South Park's No. 160 boasted a headlight and tender lamp which, combined, were almost as big as its cab. On the page opposite, two C&S narrow gauge business cars are shown at Half Way Tank on the east approach to Boreas Pass and (BELOW) No. 70 takes water at Georgetown in the year 1938.

TWO PHOTOS: E. J. HALEY COLLECTION

WESTERN COLLECTION

RICHARD KINDIG

Narrow gauge operations in the Rocky Mountains have always had their share of wrecks due in part to the nature of the terrain involved and in part to the pioneer atmosphere which was inseparable from three-foot commerce. The snowy landscape at the right is an aerial view, taken in January, 1948, of all that was left of the D&RGW's last name passenger train, *The San Juan*, near Chama when a mighty avalanche, loosened by the passage of the engine and cars, carried the entire train hundreds of feet down the mountainside without injury to crew or passengers. BELOW: a minor contretemps on the Colorado Central at Central City attracts a modest gathering of sidewalk superintendents at about the turn of the century.

WESTERN COLLECTION

THE DENVER POST

Another and more serious interruption in the conduct of the affairs of the Colorado Central took place on the Boulder branch of the line near Boulder when a flange on the tender broke as CC No. 60 was backing up and precipitated the engine upside down into the bed of Clear Creek. The locomotive cab was flattened like a collapsed opera hat and both engineer and fireman severely injured. The road was under Union Pacific management at the time, and the combine shown at the left of the picture, was UP No. 1322.

RICHARD KINDIG COLLECTION

MURIEL S. WOLLE

OTTO KUHLER

RICHARD KINDIG

At Jefferson, depicted on the page opposite, long after the railroad's abandonment, by the distinguished artist, Muriel Wolle, stock raising was the principal industry and many a carload of beef critters went out of there in the eighties on the South Park's stock cars. BELOW: Otto Kuhler, the equally distinguished industrial designer, depicts at Jefferson a ground blizzard sweeping down from Kenosha Pass in the Tarryall Mountains, a sort of fierce snow squall that rages close to the earth and seldom higher than a man's shoulders. On this page, in the closing days of the High Line at Boreas Pass, the Colorado & Southern's No. 58 headpins the clean-up train, a gentle cloud of coal smoke waving a wistful farewell from its stack that was locally known as a "beartrap."

NARROW GAUGE MUSEUM

Although votes for women were not generally contemplated in 1912, it was evident that baggage smashing, at least along the South Park, was not altogether a masculine privilege. The husky woman in a leather apron hoisting the Saratoga aboard the buckboard, while somebody's sister in city attire looks on, was the South Park's passenger agent and baggage master at South Platte depot and she also had the morning mail to get on the road. The tracks curve toward Ultima Thule, and the carry-alls and their patient horses wait in a homely and nostalgic scene of country railroading when the motor car was still a rich man's toy. BELOW: is a catastrophe along the Greeley, Salt Lake & Pacific, near Sunset, with the Union Pacific, Denver & Gulf's No. 154 standing by with a relief train.

RICHARD KINDIG COLLECTION

WESTERN COLLECTION

At the Forks of Clear Creek long ago, this locomotive of the Colorado Central, later to be combined with the original South Park in the operating economy of the Colorado & Southern, posed on the track leading from Idaho Springs and Georgetown. The track at the right is the narrow gauge mainline to Blackhawk and Central City and all the "Little Kingdom of Gilpin."

TWO PHOTOS: BENJAMIN DRAPER COLLECTION

Correctly attired in bowler hat, wing collar, and dark business suit, and seated on a handcar which carried the photographic equipment of L. C. McClure who took this picture, is Arthur Chapman, author of *Out Where the West Begins* and a noted authority on Colorado antiquities. The track is that of the narrow gauge Argentine Central near its high altitude terminal at Waldorf. In the distance is the wagon road over Argentine Pass en route to the mines of Summit County and, eventually, Leadville. Nearby was the Waldorf Mine itself, whose rich production of silver over the years financed the building of the Argentine Central by Edward John Wilcox for whom, years after the railroad had become only a memory, Mt. Wilcox was named and a tablet unveiled at Waldorf, by now a ghost town where once the three-foot rails had ended.

The narrow gauge Argentine Central Railroad running to the summit of Mt. McClellan connected with the Colorado & Southern's Clear Creek line through the intermediate agency of the three-foot rails of the Georgetown, Breckenridge & Leadville, whose eight-and-a-half mile right of way achieved world fame for its inclusion of the Georgetown Loop. The Argentine Central, which took off from the GB&L's track near the Silver Plume Pavillion was the brain child of Edward John Wilcox, an early-day mining man, and was designed to lead to the mouth of the Wilcox Mining Tunnel at Waldorf, sixteen miles from its C&S connection at Silver Plume, and Shay geared engines were the original motive power on the run. When the line was completed to Waldorf in 1906, the Post Office located there at timber line was said to be the highest in the United States with an elevation of 11,666 feet, and the Colorado & Southern's publicity department was quick to exploit the scenic wonders of the Argentine Central as an incentive to tourist travel on the Clear Creek cars. Three years after the Argentine's completion at a cost of $300,000, Wilcox sold out for $44,000 and in 1912, the property again changed hands, this time for $5,000. It was torn up in 1919 for scrap. The illustration at the left is from a contemporary C&S pamphlet, while (BELOW) the high girders of the once marvelous Georgetown Loop still tower over the mutations of time in a photograph by L. C. McClure.

TWO PICTURES: WESTERN COLLECTION

OTTO PERRY

The Teller House in Central City, forty miles out of Denver up Clear Creek, opened for business in June of 1872, and in September of the same year, the Colorado Central Railroad started laying narrow gauge track up Clear Creek Canyon out of Golden where it connected with the carrier's standard gauge. Central City had already donated a spike of solid gold as evidence of its faith as the eventual terminal of the Central, and everyone felt that the presence of the Teller House could be nothing but an added inducement to expedite the laying of track to bring custom to its splendid portals. Everything about the Teller House was ostentatiously elegant, which was the favorite descriptive adjective of the period. "Its parlors are perfect marvels of elegance," said the *Central City Register* at its opening. "They are elaborately furnished with the latest approved styles of walnut and damask, and carpets of finest Brussels. The piano—a Knabe square grand—has great volume and richness of tone, its strings clear and resonant as the finest Steinway . . . Each apartment door is provided with a patent safety lock, and guests may therefore lay down to peaceful slumbers, undisturbed by apprehensions of getting their heads blown off or valuables lifted by burglars . . . In the event of fire, occupants of each floor can be emptied out onto terra firma by rear exits as rapidly as any reputable person could desire . . . Bathrooms and water closets will be placed on the second and third floors, the first for gentlemen, the latter for ladies." For the grand opening, E. E. Barnum's Cornet and String Band was lured away from the Long Island Sound Steamers of Jim Fisk. In its time and place, the Teller House went strictly first class. For nearly seven decades, the little trains of the Colorado Central and subsequently of the Colorado & Southern, as shown above, brought names that made news to Central and the Teller. On the page opposite, an early-day freight pauses for its portrait at Beaver Brook on the way up to Blackhawk and Central, where the company thoughtfully maintained a water tank for its engines and a bar for the sluicing of its animate freight.

One of the most sensational romances of the Old West had its setting in part at the Teller House at Central City where Lieutenant Governor H. A. W. Tabor kept his mistress, Baby Doe, born Elizabeth McCourt of Oshkosh, Wisconsin, in an elaborate suite whose fragile gilt furniture may be seen there to this day. The millionaire maintained another and even more sumptuous apartment for her in Denver's swaggering Windsor Hotel and when Baby Doe commuted between them, a business car on the narrow gauge down Clear Creek was always at her disposal. Later Tabor married Baby Doe but the scandal of his own divorce haunted him until his death and their June-and-September love affair became part of the body of folklore of Colorado in its silver years.

CENTRAL CITY REGISTER-CALL

WESTERN COLLECTION

Long since buried, perhaps in a form of obscure symbolism, by the tailings of the mines it served is the Colorado & Southern's once substantial stone depot at Central City. Waiting room and ticket grille, baggage master's office and telegraph bay alike await Judgment Day beneath the debris of time, one with the various cities of Troy, with Pompeii, perhaps with the sunken mystery of Atlantis. It may be that in years to come and in the stations and terminals of a vanished America, archaeologists of the future will imagine the temples of a great national religion, and they will be right, for once the railroads were in a very real way the true faith of the American people, a way of life and a believing all its own. Far from vanished, however, is Central City itself, and every summer thousands of visitors roll in automotive comfort up from Denver to see where the miners gloried and drank deep in the Teller House and tossed minted gold to players on the opera stage. They, too, and in their way will be successors to a vanished race of nabobs, for their wheels will still follow along the edges of Clear Creek, the right of way where once the steamcars ran. On this page two drawings by Muriel Wolle perpetuate the memory of the C&S depot in other years.

TWO DRAWINGS: MURIEL S. WOLLE

One of the rarest of narrow gauge collector's items, the Denver, Boulder & Western Railroad operating up Boulder Canyon out of Boulder started life as the thirteen mile Greeley, Salt Lake & Pacific in 1882. Its terminus was at Sunset and its end of operations came in 1894 when almost its entire length was washed out in a cloudburst. In 1898 its right of way was relocated at a more prudent elevation and the new company organized as the Colorado & North Western with another thirteen miles of track from Sunset to Ward and a twenty-three mile branch to Eldora. In 1909 the C&NW went into receivership and emerged as the Denver, Boulder & Western under which style it operated until its abandonment in 1919. Advertised as "The Switzerland Trail of America" for its scenic wonderments, the C&NW motive power included four Consolidations, a Mogul, a Shay and a Climax and there were fifteen passenger cars, ninety-eight freight carriers and two cabooses. Tourist business flourished in winter aboard snowball and sledding trains and in more clement weathers in the form of wildflower excursions, but freight was scarce throughout the history of the three successive companies. Shown here is the road's No. 30 as it was delivered in 1898 to the Colorado & North Western by Brooks of Dunkirk with the C&NW insigne on its tender. After the abandonment of the DB&W in 1919, No. 30 went to the South Park where it saw service for years over Kenosha, Boreas and Freemont Passes and, with the demise of the South Park it went to the Rio Grande Southern. Possessed of the almost unique distinction of having had three narrow gauge carriers shot from under its drivers, No 30 today is on permanent exhibit at Boulder with a Denver & Rio Grande Western coach and a Rio Grande Southern caboose on its drawbar. The fine action painting by Howard Fogg shows No. 30 on the highline west of Sunset with a glimpse of the Great Plains reaching away below and at the left of the picture.

CHARLES CLEGG

From Hangtown in the Mother Lode to the Coeur d'Alene, and from Last Chance Gulch to Tombstone, every mining town in the Old West worth its cooking salt boasted a "French Louis," whose Parisian accent and reputedly classic cuisine lent *ton* and prestige to the diggings. Pattern and prototype of all French Louis' was Louis Dupuy, proprietor of Georgetown's Hotel de Paris, first citizen of this remote community and an eccentric of legendary proportions. Dupuy was not his real name and he was a deserter from the U. S. Army, but from 1875 until his death in 1900, the culinary resources of the Hotel de Paris made Colorado history. Every visiting celebrity, from Mme. Franziska de Janauschek, the Polish actress on tour in "Mary Stuart" and "Bleak House," to Lord Dunraven and Eugene Field, made safari to Georgetown to try the mushroom omelette at the Hotel de Paris and engage in philosophical discourse with Louis. They came up Clear Creek aboard the plush-and-mahogany steamcars of the Colorado Central from Denver, and dined in gaslit splendor off antelope steak and soufflé of Eastern oysters which had arrived packed in iced brine on the same train, and they skirmished mightily with the finest cellars of claret and Burgundy between Potter Palmer's Hotel in Chicago and the Palace in San Francisco. Over the Rainwater Madeira and 1811 cognac, they listened to Louis quote from Racine and Molière. A trip to the Hotel de Paris was educational and something to mark with a star in the diaries which everyone kept in those days when travel was something to talk about when one got home.

WESTERN COLLECTION

In the seventies, when ore from the Anglo-Saxon Lode assaying $23,000 a ton was bringing stability and English capital into the district, Georgetown was the third city of Colorado, only Central City and Denver being larger. Trains of the Colorado Central, such as that on the left, carried world notables on the sixty-mile, half-day trip to Silver Plume, where they lunched at the Pavillion and then stayed on to dine with French Louis in Georgetown. BELOW: at a somewhat later period, excursion trains of the Colorado & Southern followed the same rails up the sometimes turbulent South Fork of Clear Creek.

BENJAMIN DRAPER COLLECTION

LIFE © ALBERT FENN

In August, 1943, the eyes of the nation were more generally turned to events in the South Pacific, where the United States had a war on its hands, but a handful of interested persons assembled at Climax for the last narrow gauge run into Leadville of the Colorado & Southern, heir and repository of the once far-flung Denver, South Park & Pacific Railroad. Present was the Mayor of Leadville, a reporter from the Associated Press, Robert Rice, a vice-president of the C&S, A. C. Kalmbach of *Trains* magazine, and photographer Albert Fenn of *Life*, who took this photograph of the last moments of the South Park's life. The last train between Leadville and Denver had picked up its orders in 1937, and now the fourteen miles between the carbonate citadel and the molybdenum mines at Climax at the top of Fremont Pass were relaid to standard gauge.

LIFE © ALBERT FENN

Fifty-seven years of narrow gauge operations into Leadville ended when the Colorado & Southern ran its last scheduled passenger train from Leadville to Denver on April 10, 1937. Almost at the last, No. 8 is shown pausing with the two-car varnish haul at Baker Tank. It put an end to the long legend of overnight Pullmans from the Colorado capital to Leadville and Gunnison, carrying whiskered miners and carbonate kings in broadcloth to golden destinies. After the abandonment of 1937, attempts were made to reorganize the South Park by a handful of on-line communities, but the price of scrap steel was too high and the railroad passed into memory. At the left and on another last run, the crew of C&S No. 76 climb to their cab to take the train shown on the page opposite on its final trip from Climax to Leadville in 1943.

COLLECTION E. T. MEAD, JR.

TWO PHOTOS: RICHARD KINDIG

The South Park depot at Grant's in Platte Canyon, in 1938, presents a scene of ruin and desolation for the camera of Richard Kindig, while (BELOW) and three years later, a Colorado & Southern narrow gauge ore train heads both factually and metaphorically into the sunset at the entrance to Clear Creek Canyon a few miles west of Golden.

OPPOSITE: LIFE © ALBERT FENN

RICHARD KINDIG COLLECTION

Florence and Cripple Creek

The Florence & Cripple Creek Railroad, serving the Cripple Creek mining district and connecting in the Arkansas Valley with the Denver & Rio Grande at Florence, was the last narrow gauge railroad construction in Colorado to conform to the conventional and established pattern of three-foot carriers built for the primary purpose of achieving bonanzas in precious metals. The Uintah, built more than a decade after the Florence & Cripple Creek along the Utah-Colorado marches, was a sport in the biological sense; it did not conform to the gold and silver pattern of the narrow gauges that had gone before it but deviated to transport gilsonite. The Florence & Cripple Creek was the last slim gauge in the classic manner of the South Park, the Rio Grande Southern, the Mears short lines, and the prototypal D&RG. Its objective was basic, a traffic in ores that produced the ultimate and tangible wealth of gold.

Before the region on the far side of Pike's Peak from Colorado Springs and north of the Arkansas valley turned up the last of the Colorado bonanzas and the last great gold rush in the continental United States, saving only those to Tonopah and Goldfield in Nevada, it had been primarily a cattle grazing land of ranches and upland pastures, and when a calf belonging to one of its primeval settlers had tried to jump a stream and broke its leg in the process, its owner, Levi Welty, named the rivulet "Cripple Creek." The name was to have resounding implications of grandeur, infamy, violence, and lasting wealth before the century was over.

Gold was discovered in the shadow of Mount Pisgah by a rancher known as Cowboy Bob Womack in 1890, and before Cripple Creek was to run its eventual course and become one more Rocky Mountain ghost town, it was to see the meeting of the Old West and the new day of technology, the grizzled pick and burro prospector and the high-pressure stock promoter, the Ames shovel and the long lines telephone. Here, in dusty confusion, the last of the Colorado bonanzas erupted in sudden wealth of staggering proportions, labor warfare, social splendor, and the greatest publicization ever accorded a mining camp. Cripple Creek had everything that had been part of the great bonanzas before it at Virginia City, the Mother Lode, the Coeur d'Alene, Alder Gulch and Tombstone and it also had stock tickers, the Western Federation of Miners, Spencer Penrose and Bert Carlton, Apperson Jack Rabbit motor cars, Julian Street, Texas Guinan, silk hats and evening dress. It was a heady admixture.

Although Morris Cafky, a fellow-toiler in the vineyard of railroad folklore, waxes fairly lyrical over the "vision and ability" of David Moffat in laying out and building the F&CC, it would seem in the light of hindsight that the construction of a railroad to Cripple Creek was fairly obviously indicated in 1893, and it may also be doubted if the F&CC was either inspired in its location or prudently built. Two other carriers, both standard gauge, followed hard on the heels of the narrow gauge, almost immediately began subverting its traffic, and both outlived it. The reason for their supremacy lay almost entirely in their location. Both the Midland Terminal and the Colorado Springs & Cripple Creek District Railway converged on Mount Pisgah directly from the Springs, where they connected not only with the D&RG, but also with the Colorado & Southern, Rock Island and the Santa Fe, and both were closer to Denver by many miles than via the F&CC's circuitous connecting with the D&RG through Florence, Pueblo and the Springs.

But while the F&CC eventually became an also-ran in the contest for Cripple Creek traffic and dividends, from the outset and to this day it had an inside track to sentiment and the human heart, for it was narrow gauge. Its three-foot dimension was an asset for immortality possessed by none of the competition.

Following the immemorial pattern of prospecting in the Old West, Cowboy Bob Womack sold his claim for peanuts to more sophisticated operators who took millions from it. He was in the best tradition of the discoverers of precious metals. The four pioneers of the mighty Comstock Lode all died in poverty, one by his own hand. The desert rats who uncovered Eureka, Central City, Goldfield, Rhyolite, Bodie and countless other first-comers came to the same end. Almost alone of the pick-and-burro prospectors, Ed Schiefflin, discoverer of Tombstone, took a huge fortune amounting to many millions from the Lucky Cuss Mine and the Tough Nut Lode, but even he died with an estate of no more than $30,000. Cowboy Bob sold out for $500 and died of the occupational disease of stumble-bums, a cirrhosed liver. Toward the end he was known as Crazy Bob.

But Cripple Creek and its adjacent mines at Victor, Goldfield, and Elkton emerged shortly into the effulgence of a full-fledged gold rush. Two real estate promoters, Horace Bennett and Julius Meyers, platted a townsite. Fresh out of Harvard, there arrived in a wing collar and hard bowler hat young Spencer Penrose,

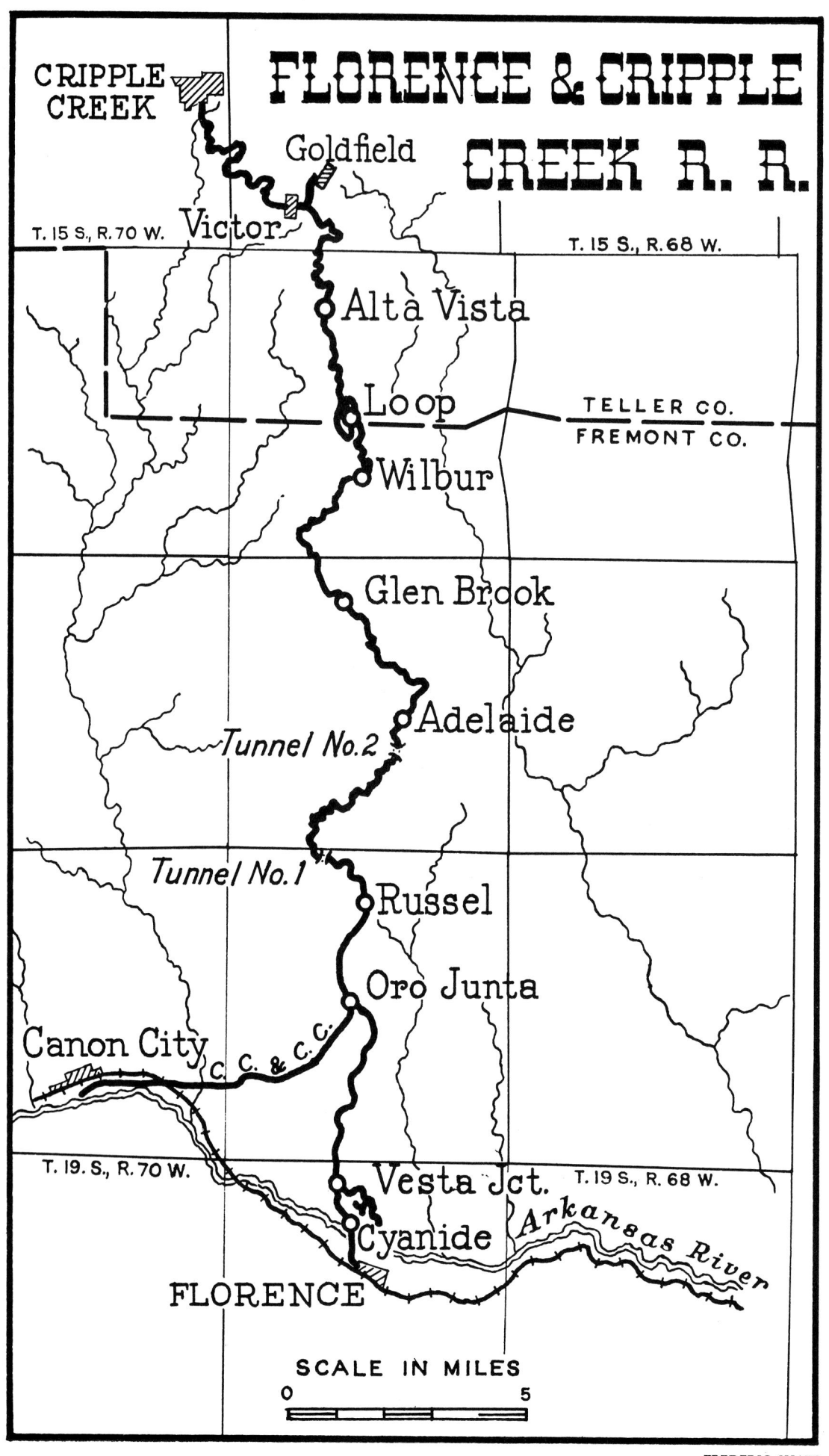

brother of Pennsylvania's princely Senator Boise Penrose, to become Colorado's greatest sport, moneybags and first citizen and eventual builder of the Broadmoor Hotel at the Springs. Hotels, saloons, dance halls, bagnios, and honky tonks reared false fronts and wooden awnings on Bennett Avenue. In 1893, the year the F&CC was started, Winfield Scott Stratton, an indifferent journeyman carpenter, hit pay dirt in the Independence Mine and became Cripple's first of a bumper crop of millionaire men.

Among the incorporators of the F&CC Railroad Company, the name of David Moffat was conspicuously missing, but he was nevertheless the moving spirit of the venture which was capitalized for $1,000,000. Narrow gauge construction was specified and logical in the light of its Florence connection since the D&RG maintained operations over three rails as far as Leadville until 1911. No trans-shipment was necessary and a good deal of Rio Grande rolling stock was diverted to the Cripple Creek traffic once the line was completed. The basic expense of grading was largely obviated by the circumstance that the survey followed the wagon tracks of what had been known as the Florence & Cripple Creek Free Road. A roundhouse and depot were built at Florence and the little line got under way with an exultant shout until it encountered an impediment of geology called Phantom Canyon. Two tunnels were blasted through inconvenient rock formations and bridges were built where the wagon road had forded Eight Mile Creek. By May of 1894, the rails were at milepost 25.3 at Wilbur, only six air-line miles from Cripple Creek. A stage line made connection with the railhead, as had been the custom on so many other Colorado railroads as they neared their objectives, and a newspaper account in *The Creede Candle* announced: "The railroad is in first class shape to Wilbur Station." In the light of subsequent developments, this could be taken as optimistic, but for the moment it was a fair enough assay.

Most spectacular portion of the F&CC construction was contained in the last six miles between the District and Wilbur, where a four per cent grade carried the tracks to Rock Point and Alta Vista over a lariat-shaped series of loops which, at one point, completely reversed the direction of the right of way and from whose topmost elevation at the ridge, the two lower levels of the loop were visible in the canyon far beneath. A passing siding was built in the intermediate level and helper engines assigned to all up-freight operations.

The first train of any sort to enter Cripple Creek was the F&CC's narrow gauge passenger run which on July 1, 1894, arrived with borrowed D&RG coaches behind an also borrowed D&RG locomotive, the diamond stacked *Chama,* which had been outshopped by Baldwin back in 1880. The customary railroad celebration ensued and only came to an inglorious end the next day, when the down train overturned on a low trestle near Anaconda and one passenger was killed. On the Fourth of July, Cripple got another railroad, the standard gauge Midland Terminal, which built into town from a connection with the Colorado Midland's mainline at Divide.

The presence of two railroads, to be joined in a few years by a third carrier, the Colorado Springs & Cripple Creek District standard gauge, produced varying schools of thought in Colorado financial circles. Cassandra-minded prophets forecast universal ruin through too much competition. Civic boosters saw ever greater prosperity as rail service increased. As it happened, the optimists were right; from the start there was traffic and to spare for both lines, and some years later, the *Denver Republican* was authority for the statement that, in 1893, the F&CC paid for its construction every three weeks. Possibly this was an exaggeration, but there can be no doubt that the little road was in clover from the beginning.

The F&CC as the first railroad to achieve Cripple Creek, albeit by a narrow margin, deserved and for a time got the cream of the camp's business both in passengers and in carloadings. In 1893 the production of gold in the district's great mines, the Portland, Cresson, Independence, Elkton and Golden Cycle reached better than $2,000,000 and from then on its wealth soared with every passing year until it reached its zenith in 1900 with $18,000,000. In that period the population, too, had increased until there were an estimated 30,000 permanent residents in Cripple Creek and its surrounding communities. Such a concentration of money and people in a region that less than a decade before had been little more than an upland pasture and in an age when no other considerable overland transport was available implied good times for the railroads and the F&CC in its modest way proved a bonanza in keeping with the mines it served.

The road operated three passenger trains each way on a daily schedule over the forty miles between Cripple and Florence. The equipment was leased from the D&RG and included, in addition to the conventional coaches and combines, through Pullman buffet cars between Denver and the District. The little varnish cars, *Ogden, Provo, Salida, Salt Lake* and *Cimarron,* boasted ten sections and a kitchen compartment, ornate coal oil lamps and Baker heaters, a patent furnace whose eccentric conduct bemused and baffled train crews for years on runs where through steam lines from the engines were impracticable. In 1895 the narrow gauge showed a net of $37,000 which, if not comparable to the earnings of such haughty bonanzas as the Virginia & Truckee out Nevada way, was still nothing to sneeze at.

In the fall of 1895 when the F&CC had been in useful and practicable operation for little more than a year, the forces of nature demonstrated that the economies practiced in the line's construction were of a very costly nature in the end. An evening cloudburst sent a flash flood roaring down Eight Mile Creek "eclipsing the high water mark made in the canyon since the Arkansas Valley has been inhabited by white people." Twelve miles of F&CC track were completely destroyed in places where prudence would have dictated its location at a substantially higher level. Just how costly the original economy had been was demonstrated when an outlay of nearly $200,000 was necessitated in relocating the tracks through Phantom Canyon at a level that was considered above any possible flood line and proved so for sixteen years to come.

The next regional disaster was freighted with grief for many but not for the narrow gauge. In the spring of 1896 Cripple Creek itself burned with a great burning and in a space of five or six hours was as flat as a collapsed opera hat. A few days later a second conflagration incinerated whatever structures, either public or private, had escaped the original holocaust. The flames had their origin in a characteristic Western manner when a bartender and a prostitute quarreled in the Central Dance Hall and overset a coal oil lamp. In the course of the fire, the boilers in the furnace room of the Palace Hotel, the town's most aristocratic hostelry, exploded and maimed a score of bystanders and firefighters. Seven hundred pounds of dynamite stored among the canned goods on the shelves of Harder's Grocery were detonated, while hundreds of barrels of whisky blew up to add to the doomsday thunderclaps. Other whisky barrels in the course of being rolled to safety by saloonkeepers were overtaken by the flames and rolled blazing down the town's steeply inclined streets to spread destruction at an accelerated rate. Across the divide in Colorado Springs residents paused in their affairs to watch a huge dun colored cloud of smoke which lifted above the mountaintops. All phone and telegraph wires were down but Springs businessmen knew without being told that an emergency was at hand and relief trains started up Ute Pass over the Midland with blankets, bread and tinned goods for the stricken city.

When it was all over Cripple Creek set about rebuilding. As had been the case in Virginia City on the Comstock twenty years earlier, the mines were in fullest operation, the community was booming and there was no thought of anything but getting back into production. Virginia City had used building materials at such a rate that the legendary Virginia & Truckee in a single day scheduled forty train movements between Carson City and the side of Sun Mountain, and bricks and boards were in similar urgent requisition at Cripple Creek. The F&CC had only ten engines on its motive power roster at the time but quickly borrowed twenty more from the Rio Grande for the duration of the emergency. Extras roared up Phantom Canyon day and night and down trains of empties arrived at Florence and Canon City with brakeshoes smoking.

Cripple Creek's ill wind blew prosperity toward the F&CC.

Much time and consequently money was being lost in freighting in ores from mines in such outlying districts as Bull Hill and Altman to the loading chutes at Victor and Cripple Creek and now the owners of the F&CC consolidated their already firm grasp on a lion's share of the regional traffic by building a subsidiary narrow gauge known as the Golden Circle with spurs and stub tracks reaching out to the most distant shafts and headframes. Suburban passenger traffic was also a source of substantial revenue in this pre-motor car age, and the F&CC purchased a fast tank engine from Schenectady for the commuter trade to Independence, Altman and Vista Grande. The narrow gauge was beginning to resemble nothing so much as a branch office of the Denver Mint.

In 1899 another subsidiary, the seven miles long Canon City & Cripple Creek Railroad was built to connect the Canon City of its title with the F&CC mainline at a point north of Florence designated as Oro Junta.

But the affairs of the District were now approaching their zenith of production and competition between the F&CC and the Midland Terminal was beginning to be productive of losses to both carriers. It was an age of consolidations and mergers and tying up of loose ends and inevitably the transport pattern of Cripple Creek was headed for a monopoly. A group of capitalists from as far afield as Boston and Ontario organized a holding company incorporated as the Denver & Southwestern Railway and in its portfolio by purchase there shortly appeared the F&CC, the Midland Terminal, the Golden Circle and the Canon City & Cripple Creek. The age of wasteful competition between the District's carriers was, for a time at least, over.

Long sections of the F&CC were at once laid to heavier rail. Half a dozen new and up to the minute locomotives appeared on its roster. Parts of the Golden Circle were tracked to standard as well as narrow gauge for the accommodation of the rolling stock of both railroads. The F&CC yards now boasted nearly 300 freight cars of various sorts and sixteen of its own passenger coaches, combines and mail cars.

And most important of all a well defined operational policy governed both railroads. All local freight, ore for the smelters at Florence and Canon City and narrow gauge interchange from the D&RG was allotted to the F&CC. Freight having its origins in standard gauge territory largely to the east of the Rocky Mountains came in over the Midland's standard trackage. So far as Cripple Creek was concerned the Midland was predominantly a carrier of import, the F&CC an export line. The arrangement effected many operational economies and benefitted both railroads accordingly.

In the early days of the F&CC's profitable operations, its management adhered to the old practice of naming its locomotives after regional Colorado landmarks or individuals associated with the management of the railroad. No. 1 appropriately enough was the *Victor*, and there followed in logical succession the *Elkton, Cripple Creek, Anaconda, Florence, Sumner, W. S. Stratton, Goldfield, Alta Vista, Independence, Strong* and *Gold Coin*. These were all 2-8-0 type engines and the road's 4-6-0 locomotives were the *Portland, Isabella, Vindicator, Granite, Last Dollar* and *Vista Grande*. Sometime after the acquisition of the carrier by the Allied Lines the pleasant custom of naming the engines was suspended and thereafter only utilitarian numbers served for identification of the little iron ponies clawing their way up grade from the Valley of the Arkansas.

Lacking in the record of the last of the bonanza narrow gauges is any trace of strictly luxury equipment save for the connecting D&RG's sleeper-buffets on the overnight run out of Denver. There seem to have been no business cars and no account has been discovered by even so industrious a chronicler as Morris Cafky, the road's official historian, of any of the narrow gauge private varnish that occasionally rolled over the other Colorado slim gauges to distant mining camps and lent such romantic flavor to the personages aboard them. The F&CC was too short for this ultimate panache of administrative splendor.

The narrow gauge engines ran down the years. Mining fell off, although not calamitously in the Cripple Creek District, and a menace hitherto undreamed of began appearing on the highways of the changing West. The first automobiles around the Springs, Brush runabouts, Olds touring cars, Pope Toledos, Appersons, White steamers and primeval Cadillacs were naturally rich man's toys. Even Spencer Penrose purchased a steel gray Rolls Royce Silver Ghost I which can be seen in the Broadmoor carriage house to this day. Roads were abominable, motors and their accessories unpredictable. It didn't seem likely that any threat was posed to steam railroading generally or passenger traffic in particular.

Nevertheless passenger traffic over the F&CC seemed to melt away toward the end of the first decade of the new century. The shorter, faster, highly spectacular route of the CS&CCD was claiming the lion's share and basking in the enthusiastic approval of such notables as Theodore Roosevelt and Julian Street who wrote about it for *Collier's*. To be sure, in addition to hymning the wonderments of the Short Line, Street got himself clawed up for life in a scuffle with the embattled citizenry of Cripple Creek.

Street had been doing a series on the American scene for Mark Sullivan, then editor of *Collier's*, and during a brief encounter of an hour or so duration with the various aspects of The District had emerged in the opinion that a ponderable portion of the population were ladies of easy and strictly commercial virtue. Never a specially thorough reporter, he based his evaluation of the town on a conversation with a first citizen of Myers Avenue known as Leo the Lion, by whom he had been solicited as he emerged from a refreshment parlor, and the resulting report in *Collier's* made Cripple Creek out to be the twentieth century repository of all the collective vices of Gomorrah, Rome and Port Said in their most florid years.

If Street had been a student of Western mores and psychology he might have been warned by a remarkably similar event twenty years earlier in Virginia City whose close parallel to Cripple Creek was not limited to the operations of its short line railroad. In the course of a tour of the Old West inaugurated by Frank Leslie, proprietor of *Frank Leslie's Illustrated Weekly Newspaper*, a group of reporters had visited the then soaring community of Virginia City. Largely they had reported in glowing terms on the operation of the deep mines of the Lode which in 1875 were at the summit of production achieved at Cripple in 1900. But Mrs. Leslie, indifferent to Cornish pumps and cyaniding processes, went away from the Comstock with very much the same opinion of its civic morals that Street had of Meyers Avenue: i.e. there were more strumpets on Sun Mountain than there were ladies and she had said so right out loud in a subsequent book.

Virginia City seethed but bided its time, and Judge C. C. Goodwin, then editor of the terrible tempered *Territorial Enterprise*, hired a private operative in New York to investigate Mrs. Leslie's own past. When it transpired that she herself was an adventuress with a flaming record, the story made delightful reading in an article in the *Enterprise*, occupying the entire first page and was so popular around Nevada that the document was reprinted in pamphlet form.

The time when Street's interview with Leo the Lion appeared was one when the virtue of American womanhood was venerated to the point of physical nausea and of the Gibson Girl who froze the marrow of a cad with a stare of chaste outrage. Chastity and motherhood became such a national bore in the early nineteenth century that neither has ever completely recovered in the public trust or esteem.

Collier's circulation boomed; Cripple, like Virginia City, seethed, but not for long. Obviously it would be unprofitable to investigate Street as Judge Goodwin had investigated Mrs. Leslie. Men were different. But the feud between Cripple and *Collier's* was by now a matter of impious hilarity throughout the nation and one evening at a meeting of the county commissioners a brief statement was handed the night stringer for the Associated Press at the office of the *Cripple Creek Times*.

The name of Myers Avenue had formally and officially been changed by the city fathers to Julian Street.

Next morning Street was the laughing stock of a hundred million newspaper readers and carried the scars of his encounter with Leo the Lion to the grave.

The end came for the little F&CC in 1912 and with only nineteen years of mainline operation behind it the narrow gauge was the shortest lived of all its contemporaries in Colorado. A flash flood once again descended Phantom Canyon taking with it eighteen bridges and more or less permanently destroying nine miles of right of way. The Allied Lines management was reluctant to rebuild although operation of the mine trackage in and around Cripple Creek was uninterrupted with the four locomotives, twenty-eight boxcars and sixty-seven ore cars that were stranded at the upper end of the line. The usual hassle with the ICC ensued when Canon City applied for an injunction to force the operators to rebuild, but in the end the trackage, rolling stock and other tangibles of the once prosperous narrow gauge at the District end of its line went into the assets of its leased subsidiary, the Golden Circle Railroad.

The right of way through Phantom Canyon became briefly an automobile highway and widely admired for its scenic splendors, but the forces of nature were as hostile to internal combustion as they had been to steam expansion engines. Flash floods took out the gravel surface as regularly as they had the ballast and rails of the F&CC and, while navigable to four-wheel powered cars today, traffic isn't brisk. It can only be concluded that God never intended Phantom Canyon for a thoroughfare for human traffickings.

WESTERN COLLECTION

When, in 1896, the inevitable took place and Cripple Creek burned flat in the manner of all shack towns, one of the most spectacular elements in the conflagration was the destruction of the Palace Hotel, which not only burned but also exploded. The F&CC had by then been two years in operation, and a hastily assembled special was run from Florence with that community's fire department on flatcars, but to no avail, since Cripple Creek was largely in ashes before it arrived. A commentary on the times was the presence of 700 pounds of dynamite, which was stocked along with Bent's water biscuits and tinned salmon at Harder's Grocery on Myers Avenue and which added Fourth of July overtones to the occasion. Other explosions demolished entire blocks when the flames reached the Palace Hotel (ABOVE), the Gold Dollar, Turf Club, and Ducey's Exchange, where vast stocks of whisky were stored. Dave Moffat's Bi-Metallic Bank justified its name when it burned with such intensity that twin streams of molten gold and silver cascaded from its cash drawers and into the gutter outside. On the page opposite is shown the giant mill of the Gold Coin Mine at Victor, with high cars of the D&RG spotted on its spur track in the absence of sufficient narrow gauge rolling stock on the Florence & Cripple Creek. BELOW is L. C. McClure's often-reproduced photograph of a F&CC engine, No. 52.

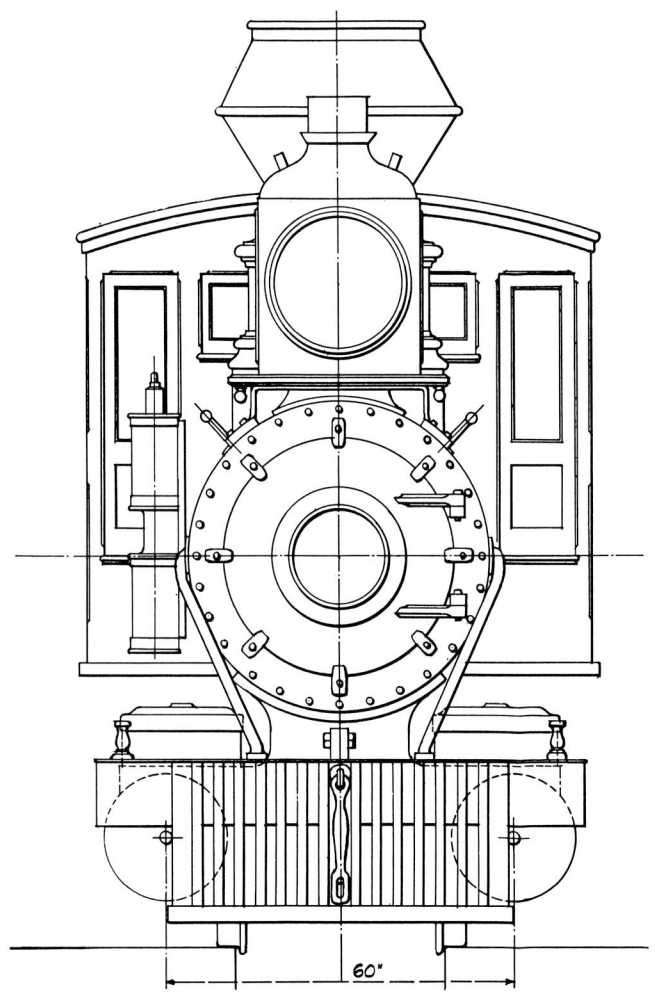

TWO PHOTOS: WESTERN COLLECTION

OTTO PERRY

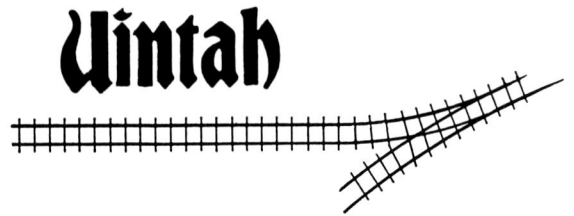

When, in 1938, the Interstate Commerce Commission allowed the abandonment of its entire seventy-two miles of narrow gauge trackage in Western Colorado and in Utah by the Uintah Railway, this *rara avis* and collector's item lived on vicariously on borrowed time under curious circumstances.

In its operating lifetime the Uintah, whose grades ranged up to seven and a half per cent, had been possessor on its motive power roster of the only two narrow gauge Mallet locomotives the record shows as having been outshopped in the United States for a common carrier. They were designed by the general manager, Lucien Sprague and built to his specifications by Baldwin in 1928, and when the Uintah closed its books they went, with modifications, to continue operations as the prime motive power of the equally narrow gauge Sumpter Valley far away in the Blue Mountains of Oregon. The Sumpter Valley enjoyed something more than local celebrity in its own right as the "Polygamy Central," having been built by Mormon capital, and the arrival of the Mallets, monsters of the three-foot iron and unique of their kind, added further to the fame and distinctive character of the lumber road. Their longevity in exile lasted for another decade after their useful life span had been concluded on the Uintah and they enjoyed a great deal of attention and even admiration during this period. They are in service to this day in Guatemala in Central America.

A number of railroads have acquired nicknames from the commodity whose transport was their principal concern. The Bath & Hommondsport in Upper York State is known as "The Champagne Route." Various West Virginia carriers are designated as coal haul railroads. On this basis the Uintah would have been known as "The Gilsonite Road," since its greatest revenue loads were of this asphaltine mineral found in the Uintah Basin and used extensively in the manufacture of paints, roofing, printers' inks and insulating compounds. The road was incorporated in 1903 and early in 1905 the first fifty-three miles of track from Mack on the mainline of the Rio Grande to Dragon were placed in service. The operation was largely financed by Colorado capitalists among the more notable of whom was Bert Carlton who had become wealthy in the Cripple Creek bonanzas and who, in common with his friend, Spencer Penrose, was now seeking new and profitable investments in Utah mines of non-precious metals.

The Uintah was all grade. Its right of way ranged north and west from the Rio Grande at Mack, over the highest point on its profile, 8,437 feet at Baxter Pass, crossed into Utah at milepost 50 and came to its terminal at Watson, sixty-two miles from where it started. The balance of its mileage was accounted for by branch lines to mines at Dragon and Rainbow. Although its engines and cars were on some sort of grade running upward from one per cent most of the time, the prize exhibit of the railroad was an incredible five miles south of Baxter Pass of constant seven and a half per cent rise. The grade was achieved over a bewilderment of loops, swirls and hairpin turns, the most abrupt of which was 66 degrees, and crews who had worked head-end or braked on the Uintah smiled tolerantly at mountain railroading elsewhere. They had taken graduate degrees.

Obviously, if such grades were available at all to adhesion motive power, it would have to be in the form of geared locomotives and the Barber Company, in whose name the railroad was incorporated, promptly ordered three Shays from Lima and purchased two more at second hand from neighboring roads while the Shays were being delivered. There was also ordered a new Baldwin Consolidation and two saddle-tank engines for use in passenger service. Nos. 50 and 51, the Sprague designed 2-6-6-2's were still twenty years in the future. The Shays were good for sixty tons on the ruling grade and the little passenger ponies ran at capacity when coupled to a single well filled combination car.

Despite its geographic location almost midway between two of the largest population centers in the West at Salt Lake and Denver, the terrain covered by the Uintah was uncommonly remote and lonely. The stations listed on the time card, Atchee, Wendella, Sewell and Rainbow Junction with the exception of Atchee where the company shops were located and also the carrier's only supply of water, were largely passing tracks in the sage, a loading platform and the shanties of maintenance-of-ways gangs. Denver papers were usually four days old by the time they reached Watson at the northern end of the run, this despite the fact that a daily round trip with an engine and single coach was scheduled from Dragon to Mack. The Rio Grande's varnish trains ran grandly through Mack without stopping or even acknowledging its existence on the map. Anyone who wanted to get to Vernal took a horse drawn stage from Dragon and all along the Uintah right of way it was possible to turn back the page of history to a time when the West was both inaccessible and authentically wild. Coal for the road's engines was produced from company owned mines at Carbonera and tenders were spotted at the mine shaft and fueled with coal which only a few minutes previously had been buried in geologic time. Water for all purposes came from Atchee and was tanked to points along the three-foot iron all the way from Watson to Mack.

Odds and ends of motive power comprised the Uintah roster in its early years, consolidations, Shays and saddletanks deriving from obscure origins in service elsewhere, in the case of one consolidation as far away as Venezuela. A Mikado purchased in 1911 from Baldwin was found to be completely unable to run over the Big Hill under its own power because of its long wheel base. At Atchee the Mike was dismounted from its pony and trailing wheels and elevated on a pair of tender trucks with its drivers hanging in mid-air and hauled over the mountain by three Shays. From that day until the road was abandoned it never saw service east of Baxter Pass.

Passenger equipment on the Uintah would have delighted the student of railroad antiquities. One of its combines was built at the Atchee shops in spare time and flaunted an eccentric elegance that made it a museum piece while still in serviceable operation. Two other passenger cars were old Rio Grande sleepers that had once been on the Denver-Salt Lake run when that entire system was narrow gauge and they retained an atmosphere of seedy grandeur until they ended up their days as outhouses in the surrounding countryside.

Freight cars were company built and so was one of the Shays. The master mechanic discovered he had so large a supply of spare parts for the existing Shays at Atchee that he had practically a complete locomotive lacking only a boiler. The Lima Company welded a boiler back in Ohio and No. 7 was run up from findings in the company shops.

In 1928 there came to the Uintah's motive power roster the first of the two locomotives that were to give the railroad a special flavor and cachet of distinction in its declining years. They were a product of the genius for solution of seemingly insoluble problems of Lucien C. Sprague, at the time general manager of the railroad and later celebrated on a national scale for his rehabilitation of the faltering destinies of the Minneapolis & St. Louis Railway. For the Uintah the Baldwin Locomotive Works outshopped a high pressure articulated engine with 2-6-6-2 wheel arrangement with 42,000 lbs. tractive force and a ratio of adhesion of 4. 62. Water was carried in a pair of tanks on either side of the boiler and fuel was bituminous coal with 82 per cent of the total weight of the engine resting on the twelve driving wheels.

The Sprague engines were a success of resounding proportions. They marched up and down the Uintah's seven and a half per cent grades and around sixty-six degree curves with an aplomb that delighted the management and made motive power history so far as the narrow gauge was concerned. Legend in Colorado has it to this day that when the first of the Uintah's articulateds was delivered, the builders had chosen to disbelieve Mr. Sprague's specifications for a seven and a half per cent ruling grade on the basis that no such railroad existed and had inclined the crown sheets to compensate for no more than a six per cent grade with the result that when the engine first started up the hill at Moro Castle there was no water at one end of the crown sheet. This may well be apochryphal and in any event the articulated was soon joined by another built to identical specifications where boiler water covered the crown sheet at all times as God obviously intended it to do.

When at last highway trucks proved more economical for the removal from its source of the gilsonite that had been the Uintah's principal and indeed almost only source of revenue and the carrier closed its books, the two articulated locomotives, still in the prime of their youth and usefulness went into service on the Sumpter Valley Railroad running out of Baker, Oregon, where it connected with the Union Pacific. For their reincarnation under the Big Sky the Baldwins were stripped of their saddle type tanks and fuel was carried in a conventional trailing tender which was sometimes supplemented with an auxiliary water tank car.

The Sumpter Valley, or Polygamy Central of local usage, had been built in the spacious days of log cutting in the Blue Mountains and Strawberry Mountains of Oregon, and its three-foot tracks ran for miles along the Powder River in the shade of the giant spruces which furnished its main source of revenue from Bates to Baker by way of Sumpter. In earlier times it had carried a flourishing passenger trade in salmon colored coaches and the mails in Railway Post Office cars, but by the time the Uintah articulateds arrived, its sole traffic was in milled lumber which went out to the great world through interchange with the Union Pacific's Oregon mainline at Baker. There the Sprague engines lived out their extended lease on life, snorting valiantly on the grades and tossing smoke plumes against the summer sky visible for miles around. To the end they enjoyed a wide celebrity as the only narrow gauge common carrier Mallets in North America and their profiles are recorded for posterity in the films of scores of admirers of their exotic, albeit pastoral operations.

On a railroad of such precipitous grades and generally forbidding terrain as the Uintah there were naturally accidents but because of the limited passenger traffic over its company trackage these were almost always of a self-contained and, as it were, family nature involving employees and never approaching the proportions of catastrophe that would have been inevitable had the Uintah's trains had any great concentration of passenger business.

Operating rules demanded that all brakes be inspected and tested at Baxter Pass before commencing the descent of the Big Hill and again at Atchee on the up-run. A brakeman rode the last car in all trains at all times and schedules called for fifty minutes time between Atchee and Baxter Pass, a matter of only six miles, and forty minutes for the seven miles from Baxter Pass to Wendella. Nobody set any speed records when the schedule was observed but occasionally trains got out of hand and some hair raising speeds were achieved on curves usually negotiated at a decorous five miles an hour.

In the winter of 1917, No. 20 was descending the Big Hill with a single combine for its train when the brakes failed to hold and the two units shot off as gravity dictated until the engine left the rails and rolled down a mountainside for a distance of 500 yards turning over and over as it went. The conductor, who had been setting up hand brakes on the front platform of the combine, was killed. The engineer was seriously injured but the passengers, all of whom were men and company employees, jumped before the speed was excessive and sustained no more than the conventional contusions and cuts. On another occasion a Shay whose line shaft had become disconnected from the front trucks got away and rolled more than 800 feet down the mountainside to the detriment of its appearance and effectiveness. But risks were all in the day's work and never seemed to affect the morale of the sixty or seventy employees who remained on the payroll for years on end.

Life could never be said to be dull along the Uintah and if runaways were reduced to a minimum, there were other excitements in the form of minor conflagrations, picnics, and the problem of snow removal after Colorado's legendary blizzards.

Gilsonite in the form it is shipped for refinement and commercial adaptation, is highly inflammable and the Uintah carried it sacked and stacked several hundred sacks to a flat car and open to the elements. Occasionally the desert slip stream would bear a blazing cinder from a locomotive stack and deposit it where it would do the most good amongst the burlap sacks half a dozen flatcars back. If the train was on a comparatively level stretch of track where it could be braked to an immediate halt, steps could be taken to confine the flames, but if it happened on a grade where braking was out of the question for some distance, the resulting pyrotechnics could assume Paine's fireworks proportions before they were extinguished.

Clearing the tracks of snow during winter months was not altogether a pedestrian occupation. No known rotary could negotiate the Uintah's 7.5 per cent grades or sixty-six per cent curves and two or three Shays in tandem usually powered a wedge plow of primeval design where the drifts were deepest. The spreader that followed the plow had to be operated at considerable speed and spreader crews who were carried away with enthusiasm for making the snow fly in butterfly patterns on either side of the track were known to be carried right off into thin air where the track curved abruptly above a precipitous abyss.

Determined seekers after premeditated thrills sometimes rode the pilot beam of the articulated engines which thrust out a substantial distance over the brink of the mountain on sharp curves while the wheels quartered inward to follow the lay of the track.

Once, and briefly, the Uintah knew intimations of the big time and cherished ambitions to become part of a standard gauge system of continental dimensions. Its ownership was largely interlocking with that of the Colorado Midland in the persons of Bert Carlton and his associates and in the middle years of the 1914 war, a scheme was projected by which the Uintah would become a link in a through Midland route to Utah. All tie replacements between Wendella and Watson and Mack and Atchee were made with full length standard gauge ties with an eye to widening the road for conventional operations. But before the plan could come to fruition, a hysterical wartime railroad commission ordered the abandonment of the entire Midland system and the chance that standard Pullmans and transcontinent freight might one day smoke opulently through State Line and Country Boy went glimmering.

Announcement in 1938 of the impending abandonment of the Uintah even as the clouds of war were gathering on the horizons of Europe, came as a surprise to most of Colorado which viewed with dismay the passing of one more of its once numerous narrow gauge carriers. The gilsonite deposits at Rainbow, the management said, had been exhausted and new sources of the mineral which had been uncovered to the north were handier to the Moffat connection at Craig. Gone, save for a few vestigial traces of grade, is the Uintah from the face of the land, but here and there at Mack and in neighboring communities along the Rio Grande mainline its narrow gauge combines and passenger cars are still in service as tool sheds, chicken coops and summerhouses. Unshipped from their trucks and fixed for all time in the elemental Colorado landscape, they are a good deal safer for survival than ever they were as the crew tied down the hand brakes and hoped for the best on the seven per cent grade at Moro Castle.

The Uintah's No. 12 came to the Gilsonite Road from the Florence & Cripple Creek and later went on to service in the final years of the Eureka & Palisade narrow gauge serving Ruby Hill over Nevada way. The lower photograph, taken at Baxter Pass in 1912 suggests why the Great Northern's legendary symbol of a mountain goat would be equally appropriate to the heraldry of the Uintah.

TWO PHOTOS: MOODY RAILROAD PHOTOS

WESTERN COLLECTION

Scheduled passenger service on the Uintah was regularly assigned to tank engines such as shown in the photograph at the top of the page, but the carrier also had on its motive power roster a pair of 2-8-0 engines with diamond stacks that had been outshopped for the Rio Grande back in the eighties and one of them No. 11, is shown on the connecting track at Mack, where the narrow gauge met the transcontinental iron of the Denver & Rio Grande. The date of the little mixed train is not known, but it was late enough to make a diamond stack locomotive an interesting anachronism to some forgotten cameraman.

WESTERN COLLECTION

JACK THODE COLLECTION

The stretch of track that on any mainline carrier would be known as Horseshoe Curve was, of course, on the narrow gauge designed "Muleshoe," and this was the Muleshoe Curve at Morro Castle on the Uintah, where the grade was seven-and-a-half per cent and the curve ran to sixty-six degrees. On it is depicted one of the Shay engines, with a maximum tonnage rating of three coaches, and two narrow gauge boxcars spaced between. In the photograph below, a Shay is shown on the smoky end of a stock extra running downgrade toward Dragon. Occasional cattle-and-sheep movements constituted the only important traffic on the Uintah other than the gilsonite that was its main excuse for existence.

OTTO PERRY

Purists, in the Uintah's lifetime, liked to point out that its two most famous locomotives were not actually Mallets at all, as they had four-cylinder simple engines, but the two 2-6-6-2T monsters were widely known as Mallets and the name stuck. BELOW: No. 51, with four cars of gilsonite on the head end of a mixed consist, is photographed from the lower track of a sixty-six degree curve at Baxter Pass. On the page opposite are shown the shops at Atchee, the Uintah's four-wheel bouncer and one of the road's two steel combines. Twenty years after the abandonment of the Uintah saw the passing of the trucks that had put the railroad out of business. In 1957, gilsonite was being hydraulically mined and floated in solution through a gigantic pipeline seventy-two miles long from Bonanza, Utah, to Gilsonite, Colorado, to produce high-octane fuel for Barber Oil, a subsidiary of Standard of California. The pipe saved a cool million in trucking charges yearly, produced 1,300 barrels of gasoline a day, and promised to keep the refinery busy for the next half century. Gilsonite had come a long way.

TWO PHOTOS: MOODY RAILROAD PHOTOS

THREE PHOTOS: MOODY RAILROAD PHOTOS

TWO PHOTOS: OTTO PERRY

OTTO PERRY   LUCIEN C. SPRAGUE

Some concept of the formidable sixty-degree curves and seven-and-a-half per cent ruling grades of the Uintah may be gathered from the three photographs on this and the opposite page, all taken from the same vantage point on Baxter Pass by Otto Perry in 1939, a few weeks before the road suspended operations in favor of trucking the gilsonite that was its most important traffic. They depict a mixed consist behind one of Lucien Sprague's Mallet tank engines in the last days of their spectacular operation along the Colorado-Utah border before the Uintah closed down and they were sold to the Sumpter Valley in Oregon.

RICHARD KINDIG COLLECTION

H. R. GRIFFITHS

At the top of the page opposite is a scene from the Book Cliff Railroad, one of Colorado's less-celebrated narrow gauge carriers that once operated out of Grand Junction for a distance of ten miles to coal mines at Book Cliff off to the north of town. The presence of a Shay geared locomotive suggests its formidable grades, and the young man with a boater hat and a bunch of posies who occupies the engineer's seat gives the moment a pleasantly pastoral touch. If further evidence were required as to the character of the now vanished Book Cliff, the profusion of cinders on the cab roof would indicate a very low grade of fuel. Book Cliff coal sold, as a matter of fact, for $3.50 a ton delivered and $1.50 if you carried it home in your own team, and the road's little stone station house near First and Main was for years a happy landmark in old Grand Junction. In the below photograph is one of the Uintah's far-famed Mallets as it appeared in service after the Uintah's demise on the Sumpter Valley Railroad in Oregon. Gone are the saddle tanks and in their place is a conventional tender, and the trains run over meadowland tangents that never existed in the profile of the Uintah. The Mallets were to know a still further reincarnation when, after the Sumpter Valley was shot from under their flanges, they went to Central America to see service in the banana state of Guatemala. On this page is the Uintah's No. 30, with three loaded flatcars of gilsonite showing how the sometime inflammable substance was sacked and packed, with a gilsonite mine, a mere slice cut from the hillside, from which the petroleum product was recovered.

R. A. RONZIO COLLECTION

OTTO PERRY

Rio Grande Southern

Although the parallel must end there, it is impossible for the railroad historian to ignore the similarity in the careers of Otto Mears, wagon master of the San Juan and Napoleon of the narrow gauges, and Commodore Cornelius Vanderbilt, the titan of Eastern railroading and founder of the ample destinies of the New York Central & Hudson River Railroad. Both had spent ponderable portions of their life span in other agencies of transport before turning to the iron horse; in Vanderbilt's case with steamboats; in Mears's, with toll roads and teaming. Both evolved railroad systems from their previous field of activities and as the logical expression of the changing times in which they lived. Both grew old and gray in the shadow of roundhouse and freight shed. Vanderbilt died the richest man in the United States and Mears died in barely comfortable obscurity, but both were railroaders of immense influence upon the regions touched by their lives.

Their personalities were so different that at this point the parallel between the two men must come to an abrupt terminus.

Otto Mears, diminutive, Jewish and determined, came to America from Russia at the age of ten, drifted to the Far West in gold rush days and served in the First Regiment of California Volunteers in the bloodless campaigns of Texas and New Mexico. Setting up after his discharge as a storekeeper in various frontier communities of Colorado Territory, he foresaw the inevitable surge of population into the distant regions behind the Rocky Mountains and in time became the foremost toll road proprietor and packmaster in Colorado. In those halcyon times a $5. registration fee secured for the ambitious entrepreneur a toll road charter valid for twenty years and it wasn't even necessary to file a profile of the proposed construction, only to name the towns it was to connect.

In the twenty years between 1867 and 1886, Mears constructed a full dozen major wagon roads in the southwestern mountains, all of them between the mining towns which were mushrooming with the proverbial enthusiasm of prospecting communities and many of which were in a few years to become rights of way for the narrow gauge railroads on which Colorado was to ride joyously to boom or bust.

The far-flung network of Otto Mears's toll roads included as his first venture a fifty-mile highway from Saugauche over Poncha Pass to Nathrop on the South Fork of the Arkansas where it connected with the Denver-California Gulch road through South Park. In 1871 Mears built a toll road from Saugauche to Lake City via Cochetopa Pass, Cebolla Valley and Lake Fork. From Lake Fork an extension known as the Blue Mesa Road headed west to Cimarron. There was the Animas River Road from Silverton to Lake City via Howardsville, Eureka and Forks of Animas. This was later to become the route of the Silverton Northern. One of Mears's most important toll roads that was to become the basis for the Denver & Rio Grande's first transcontinental narrow gauge between Denver and Salt Lake, was from Mears Junction via Marshall Pass to Gunnison. A twenty-seven mile trail from Dallas Divide to Telluride, was destined to become part of Mears's own Rio Grande Southern Railroad, while perhaps the most spectacular and celebrated of all the Pathfinder's projects was the Rainbow Highway between Silverton, Red Mountain and Ouray over which Mears was eventually to project but never complete his Silverton Railroad.

In addition to his road-building projects, Mears was involved in every angle of freighting and packing over the highways he, himself, had built, mapping stage routes, maintaining wagon freight service, contracting for the mails and delivering all manner of supplies to the remotest and most inaccessible diggings. He was for a number of years the largest purchaser of hay, grain and teaming animals in the Territory with thousands of oxen, mules, burros and fast horses in his stables and hundreds of drivers, teamsters, stable keepers and couriers on his payroll. At the other extreme from these vast and expensive operations was Mears's contract for carrying the government mails into Ouray from Lake City in dead of winter which he accomplished through the agency of toboggans drawn by St. Bernard dogs and guided by couriers on "Norwegian shoes," as skis were then known.

The coming of the railroads found Mears better conditioned for their acceptance and organization than any of his local contemporaries, including General Palmer. The transition from wagon master of the San Juan to Napoleon of the Narrow Gauges was an easy one.

The outstanding characteristic of the Rio Grande Southern Railroad was its complete and overwhelming improbability. Except for the evidence of photographic record, it would be possible to doubt it ever existed, and the doubt would be amply justified. Except in the extravagantly optimistic railroad thinking of the time and place, the Rio Grande Southern could never have come into being. In the biological sense of the word, it was a sport, valiant, lonely, tenacious beyond the call of duty or reason. Say its name with bugles in the lexicon of the Old West, for the Rio Grande Southern was a lost cause, an allegory of futility when it was first conceived and it ended its long, unquiet life contributing to the essence of destruction that was Hiroshima.

Perhaps in the Valhalla of railroads where the lights on the tangents are green forever, the Rio Grande Southern has achieved some measure of tranquillity and repose. They will be wholly out of character.

The railroad that David Lavender calls "The Littlest Giant" can be traced to Otto Mears's toll road philosophy in the days when he was running wagon trains out of Saugauche. Everything was against him: the elements, geography and the Denver & Rio Grande, and Mears never gave them second thought. Overcoming the impossible was a daily occurrence and when it became apparent that it was impossible to run his Silverton Railroad further than Albany and Ironton for a connection with Ouray, the Rio Grande Southern came into being.

Otto Mears's determination to achieve the mining complex represented by Ouray, Telluride and Ridgway where once his Rainbow Toll Road had already run, was not going to be defeated by the mere geographic fact of Red Mountain and the terrain impervious to railroads on its far side to the north. To be sure, his three narrow gauge roads running out of Silverton, the Silverton Railroad, the Silverton Northern and the Silverton, Gladstone & Northerly had properly ventilated some of the most inaccessible mining camps in the Uncompaghres: the Joker and the Yankee Girl, Gladstone itself, Animas Forks and the great Sunnyside Mine at Eureka. But that wasn't the point: if Ouray couldn't be achieved by an extension of the Silverton Railroad from Albany or Ironton, it could be reached by a gigantic shoo-fly 162 miles long, and that was how the Rio Grande Southern took form.

When, in years to come, men shall name the names of sparkling romance that are the lexicon of the Old West, the names that clutch at the heart and have entered the stream of the nation's consciousness, the Alamo, Tombstone, Dodge City, the Staked Plains, Santa Fe Trail, South Pass, Union Pacific, Deadwood, Wells Fargo and Virginia City, they will be well advised to include in that valiant tally, the name of Otto Mears's masterpiece, the lonely, desolate and perhaps futile but still transcendingly triumphant Rio Grande Southern Railroad.

Here were concentrated all the basic realities of mountain railroading in primeval times: the thirty-pound rail laid without ballast on the elemental earth, rights of way cleaving to ledges above the bottomless abyss, snowsheds, loops, stub switches, the little mixed train daily and the teapot locomotives driven against all probability and the elements by the old bearded eagle eyes of legend.

Frustrated past all endurance by the physical fact of the seven and eight per cent grades which were unavoidable in the Canyon of the Uncompahgre beyond Albany and Ironton, Mears clapped his silk top hat firmly on his head, set his whiskers at an angle of defiance and started all over again out of Durango, fifty miles down water on the Animas from Silverton. From its beginnings in 1890 the Rio Grande Southern was to sweep boldly westward to Mancos and Dolores and then head north again via the vast mining operations of Rico, Ophir and Telluride, up the canyon of San Miguel and across Dallas Divide to Ridgway and a connection by the Denver & Rio Grande with the Ouray of his heart's desire. It took 162 miles of engineering that staggers retrospect, of loops and snowsheds and spidery trestles and it took $9,000,000 in hard money of the nineties. It didn't prove such a lot when it was completed except to be the only railroad through 4,000 odd square miles of real estate untouched by any other carrier, but it showed the Uncompahgre Mountains that it didn't pay to come to cases with Otto Mears. The Rio Grande Southern in its own peculiar three-foot way told the geology of Western Colorado where it could head in. When Mears for the first time rode down Dallas Divide on the platform of his business car which had come all the way from Durango and saw Ridgway emerge from the mists below, he knew that nothing else in life would afford the satisfaction of the moment. He had made the Golden Journey to Samarkand.

The Rio Grande Southern Railway was incorporated in October 1889 and a separate corporation, the Rio Grande Southern Construction Company, was launched at the time in a relationship which, to the eye of history, must appear a close parallel to the kinship between the Union Pacific and the financing agency known as Credit Mobilier. Otto Mears was president of both companies and the directorate included Job Cooper, Governor of Colorado, Fred Walsen, for whom Walsenburg was shortly to be named, and John C. McNeil, president of a Denver bank and a moneybags of irreproachable probity. The chief engineers were Thomas Wigglesworth and C. W. Gibbs who had already skirmished with the Colorado landscape when they built Mears's narrow gauges out of Silverton. McNeil was treasurer of the Silverton Railroad which was a handy arrangement since its operations were to a great extent to finance the RGS, and Walsen had been Mears's partner in the construction of the Rainbow Toll Road from Ouray to Silverton.

As an interlocking directorate it was an all-star cast and it was to turn in, in the RGS, the greatest performance in the way of construction of its career.

Construction commenced simultaneously at Ridgway and Durango early in 1890. The northern division from Ridgway to Rico which included the greatest natural hazards was in charge of Gibbs, and here once more a Mears's toll road, this one between Ridgway and Telluride over Dallas Divide, was ready-graded as a right of way for the three-foot rails.

No less thrifty in building the southern end of the line was Wigglesworth. A decade previous he had made a tentative survey of a narrow gauge route for the Denver & Rio Grande from Rico along the Dolores River, via Lost Canyon to Mancos and hence across the gently rolling hills to an entry to Durango from the west. The D&RG had never made up its mind to occupy the survey and now Mears and Wigglesworth merely dusted off his old profiles for the Southern.

Six months after work began out of Durango, the five miles of track reached as far as the Porter Coal Mines and the railroad was in business as a coal haul carrier. The present town of Dolores wasn't there when the first construction gangs arrived at its site, but the community of Big Bend, a mile and a half down river, saw the light as so many other towns had seen it when the railroad approached elsewhere in the land. Big Bend's leading saloon keepers, a boarding house proprietor and a sort of primeval Cash Mercantile loaded up their businesses on stone boats and then ox teams set them down where the railroad ran at Dolores.

The advancing ends of track from north and south met in December 1891 eleven miles south of Rico and the gold spike without which no American railroad could be completed was driven to certify the last section of track in the biggest railroad shoo-fly in the world. By travelling 162 miles over the Rio Grande Southern plus the sixty-three miles represented by the Silverton Railroad and the Animas branch of the Denver & Rio Grande, it was now possible to avoid the six miles of trackless and untrackable grades from Albany to Ouray. It was a masterpiece of evasion.

The first train out of Durango, appropriately decked in bunting and patriotic heraldry, steamed out of the yards December 21, with three barrels of locally brewed beer and fifty dressed turkeys as a present from the directors with which the track layers were to celebrate the end of their labors. But the road had been in business, as noted above, for sometime. Scheduled trains had also been running for more than a year between Ridgway and Telluride, a distance of forty-five miles by way of Dallas Divide, Placerville and Vance Junction and for several months from Ridgway to Rico. Now it was possible to traverse the entire Rio Grande Southern from Ridgway to Durango. The first trains made it in two days, stopping for the night at Rico, but shortly thereafter sleeper service was inaugurated over the route and miners, whisky salesmen and tourists, one to a berth as decreed by Palmer's Law, were able to make the trip in solid Pullman comfort.

Although, paradoxically, the RGS enjoyed something like prosperity hauling coal on its southern trackage and mine supplies, cattle movements and outgoing ore from the mines of Ophir or Telluride on its northern stub during construction days, it had no sooner completed its entire length than hard times loomed. Its original financing had been through the agency of a bond issue of $4,500,000 and a similar amount in common stock and although interest on the bonds was paid until 1922, no stock dividends were ever declared in the entire history of the road. Less than two years after its completion and with Colorado mines along its right of way giving promise of a rosy future, "the crime of '93" demonetized silver and the entire West was plunged into gloom and panic. Carloadings at Rico and Telluride fell to nothing and the road went into bankruptcy. Borrasca for silver meant borrasca for the railroads associated in its production and the Denver & Rio Grande was named receiver for the Southern.

From that day on the RGS was used as a repository for all the parent's woes which could be passed on to its account, and these were many. The RGS was charged huge sums for terminal rentals, leased locomotives, shopping of rolling stock and an executive payroll top-heavy with Rio Grande management. Hand-me-down material was fobbed off on it to show a profit in the Rio Grande's special accounts and Rio Grande locomotives were rented to the subsidiary while its own motive power was allowed to remain idle and degenerate on sidings at Ridgway and Durango. With seventy per cent of the Southern's stock in its possession, the Rio Grande simply and determinedly looted the smaller road.

And yet, the Southern clattered down the years, its freight trains replacing the vanished carloadings of ore with lumber, cattle, sheep and various other agricultural products which were raised in ever increasing quantities in the San Juan region. Its daily passenger run in each direction with overnight sleepers gave way to a three times a week mixed train which was the sole passenger transport for five large counties, San Miguel, Montezuma, Dolores, La Plata and Ouray. Automobiles were not yet commonplace and if they had been Southwestern Colorado and the Utah border had no mentionable roads on which to accommodate their traffic. Bankrupted, battered and operating by the grace of God and baling wire, its trains in the ditch as often as they were on the faltering rails, the RGS was a minor miracle in that it continued to run at all.

The Southern's right of way neatly bisected the maximum precipitation area of Colorado, and the Dolores and San Miguel rivers rose and took its tracks with disastrous regularity. Landslides and snow blockades in winter suspended service over the entire run for weeks at a time. The parent Rio Grande repeatedly grasped at these calamities as the occasion for scrapping the entire RGS operation, but each time just as the axe of abandonment was about to fall, the embattled communities and industries along its right of way descended on their representatives in Washington and in Denver with banshee screams and pointed up their demands for continued service with references to approaching elections which reduced senators and assemblymen to quivering masses of nervous acquiescence. Postal contracts were renewed, tax claims to the extent of $250,000 were relinquished by the interested counties and eventually the Reconstruction Finance Corporation through a subsidiary, the Defense Supplies Corporation, ponied up $65,000 to repair tracks and bridges and pay the most pressing debts for fuel and back wages.

Accidents on even the best repaired and maintained mountain railroads were a commonplace until comparatively recent times and Colorado's transcontinental mainlines had their full share of disaster by landslide, washout, the faulty span, inept dispatching and the unthrown switch. On a makeshift railroad running over incredible heights and above abysmal crevasses, the incidence of disaster was measurably higher. Engineers and firemen perished when double headers went through spans at Butterfly and Lightner Creek. At Bilk Creek Bridge a mile below Vance Junction, a light engine went through the trestle and a following train piled on top of it fifteen minutes later. In 1925 a spectacular snowslide in the San Miguel Valley below Ophir cut two freight cars neatly out of the center of a laboring train and took them a mile down the mountainside where they remain to this day, without harming members of the crew who were at their posts in engine cab and caboose at the train's two extremities. Minor derailments were so commonplace that the dispatcher at Durango knew for a certainty when a train was more than two hours late that the crew was doing things with a re-railing frog somewhere beyond telegraphic ken. To be sure, there were telephones even in unattended stations along the line such as Lizard Head but the chances of their being in operable shape were small. All train crews made a practice of carrying emergency rations in the caboose and simply holed up for the night around the cannonball stove when further progress was impossible.

David Lavender, future ranking historian of the Colorado scene, served a youthful apprenticeship as valet to RGS stock trains. Later, he cherished memories of hardships along the line, and these became more endurable as they receded down the vistas of time.

For some years after the completion of the Southern and after the turn of the century for as long as railroad excursions were a national institution, the RGS, by reason of its impressive scenic resources, carried a maximum density of picnics, outings and civic jollifications to thrill to the passage over the spindly trestles at Ophir and pick wild flowers in the meadows above Dolores. The Telluride Cornet Band and the celebrated band from the Terrible Mine, a name which gave rise to endless corny wit, were in great requisition for these pleasant occasions and sleepers, business cars and all the coaches at the road's disposal were pooled, their ice boxes filled with beer and sandwiches and the locomotive smokeboxes draped in bunting and fraternal regalia. Often the presence of an official photographer was solicited for such occasions and Homer Reid, a Telluride drug store proprietor, for many years made a nice thing out of enlargements showing the Odd Fellows and Knights of Labor in relaxed moments draped around the pilot beam of the Southern's diamond stack engines or winding up the brakes on the platform of the last car. It was part of an America that has vanished with the mustache cup and peg topped trousers.

More sophisticated were convocations of handsomely varnished narrow gauge business cars when Buckeley Wells, general manager of the incredibly rich Smuggler-Union Mine at Telluride or other precious metal nabobs entertained New York bankers and distinguished English visitors who might become investors in Colorado properties. When such occasions brought Spencer Penrose and Bert Carlton, overlords of Cripple Creek, to Telluride, often accompanied by their friend, the fun-loving Count James Pourtales, the lights in private dining rooms at the Sheridan Hotel burned until dawn and champagne empties made kitchen middens beside the parking tracks of the Rio Grande Southern depot. At such foregatherings of the mining kings, a familiar figure was Daniel C. Jackling and it was one such festive occasion that Jackling approached Penrose and Charles MacNeill with a revolutionary scheme for the profitable and economic mining of copper, although base metals were not highly thought of in Telluride and Jackling's blueprints had been labeled "wildcat" by the influential "*Engineering & Mining Journal.* Penrose and MacNeill went along with Jackling to the extent of a few millions in Cripple Creek found-money and in the next forty-five years the Utah Copper Company mined six billion pounds of pure copper and made more and richer millionaires than Cripple Creek and Telluride combined.

One of the features of pre-automobile travel in the Rocky Mountain region was a trip around the "Narrow Gauge Circle" which was promoted by the Denver & Rio Grande in days when passenger traffic had the management's unqualified approval. Special coaches, sleepers and diners were assigned to this project and passengers disembarked from the standard gauge at Salida and started their tour with a scenic ride down the Valley Line to Alamosa, a stretch of track that included fifty-three miles of unbroken tangent in the shadow of the sawtooth peaks of the Sangre de Cristo Mountains.

From Alamosa to Durango the tour followed the still existing freight—only line south to Antonito where the tracks turned west and took leave of the Chili line southward to Santa Fe, and thence via Toltec Gorge, Cumbres Pass, Chama and Pagosa Junction to the San Juan Basin at Durango. At Toltec Gorge it stopped to pay its respects both to the incomparable chasm yawning at the far end of the tunnel and to the Garfield Memorial, erected to the memory of the martyred president who was assassinated and word of whose death arrived from the East just as an excursion train of the National Association of General Passenger & Ticket Agents arrived at Toltec. A collection was taken up and the monument emplaced upon the completion of the line to Durango.

Garfield memorials enjoyed a not inconsiderable vogue in the entire West and a similar statue was at this time dedicated at Bodie, California, for many years celebrated as the wickedest mining town of them all and the native heath of Mark Twain's "Bad Man from Bodie."

The Bodie Memorial enjoyed special overtones of irony well suited to the bad fame of the community it graced. It was in actual fact, being erected to the memory of William S. Bodie, a long dead pioneer who had discovered the Esmeralda diggings, when news came on September 20, 1881, of Garfield's passing. Literally overnight, the citizenry of Bodie decided to erase the name of the founding father and in its place next morning was that of James Abram Garfield as it stands to this day in Mono County hard by the Nevada border.

Not strictly part of the Narrow Gauge Circle at the turn of the century, many visitors elected a side trip to Silverton, even as today, to view the scary abyss of Animas from the ledge at Rockwood and, in those days at least, to sample the resources of the cellars of the Grand Imperial Hotel in Silverton, a favorite gathering place of the silver nabobs whose special brand of Bourbon was almost as famous as the scenery surrounding it.

From Durango the narrow gauge trippers continued over the Mears's road, touring the mines at Rico and pausing on the upland divide to view the rock named "Lizard Head" and at the expanse of Trout Lake before essaying the Trestles of Ophir. By long odds, the Ophir trestles were both literally and figuratively, the high point of the Narrow Gauge Circle. Legend, probably apocryphal, holds that when Otto Mears first confronted its spidery foothold against the sheer cliff that terminates San Miguel Valley, he found it more comfortable to get down from the cars and cross on foot, a practice that was imitated by the timid or merely prudent for years to come. Telluride, with its multiplicity of mines clinging far above timberline to the mountain heights surrounding the town—the Tomboy, Smuggler-Union, Liberty Bell, Bullion, Hidden Treasure, Cimmarron and Cleveland—was a must and travelers listened with awe to the tales of pack mule days when terrible snowslides decimated the mining population and rescue parties sent out to locate the missing, in turn, disappeared to be seen no more until spring disclosed the bodies of rescued and rescuers alike.

From Ridgway, where the Rio Grande Southern came to an end and connected with the D&RG, the travelers continued over the road's first transcontinental narrow gauge mainline through the Black Canyon of the Gunnison and over Marshall Pass back to Salida and the standard gauge.

By the time of the 1914 war, the automobile had commenced to make inroads upon railroad travel for purely scenic and recreational purposes and the Narrow Gauge Circle ceased to rank with Yellowstone and the Grand Canyon as one of the tourist attractions of the West. But in 1945, when time was running out for the Rio Grande Southern, the authors of this book made what was probably the last passenger tour in steam over what was left of the once celebrated three-foot circle. As guests of the parent railroad and in the company of A. E. Perlman, then its general manager and later president of the New York Central, they occupied five days with the trip from Alamosa to Ridgway and recreated for the last time the glories of narrow gauge travel in a simpler and more tranquil age.

For the last communion with vanished yesterdays the two business cars B-2 and B-7 were requisitioned and stocked with vintage wines and noble cognacs, pheasant, mountain trout and comestibles appropriate to a fond farewell. The forward car contained quarters for chef and waiter, a kitchen, kitchen offices and diminutive dining salon, the following Pullman housed microscopic staterooms each with its brass bed and toilet facilities and an observation-drawing salon with railed-in observation platform.

It seems reasonable to say, at this remove, that the grand farewell tour made some sort of history in the San Juan Basin. There were gala dinners aboard the car for banker A. M. Camp at Durango, Indian ceremonial dances performed for the visitors at Rico, a day and night in the ghostly legend-haunted precincts of wartime Telluride, dreaming of golden recoveries from the Argentine and Liberty Bell and tales of secret shafts known only to dead men that led all the way from the Hidden Treasure to the Yankee Girl the other side of the mountain. And then the last grand tour of the narrow gauge was done. The rains of Dallas Divide washed out the past as effectively as though a curtain had descended behind our going.

In its final years of decline and improvisation when the pulse of the Southern flickered weakly before ceasing forever, one of the management's devisings of economy that attracted something more than purely local attention was the type of railcar built to handle both freight and passengers the length of the line and known as The Galloping Goose. The Goose varied and had several models, but generally speaking, comprised a vast box-car-like van behind and a crowded passenger cabin forward mounted on the ancient but durable chassis of Cadillacs and Pierce Arrows that had seen better days. Equipped with flanged wheels, augmented brake systems in the form of a compressor and air brakes, and in the custody of a single operator who combined the functions of engineer, brakeman and conductor, the Geese weighed only a fraction of the tonnage of a conventional steam train, required a minimum crew and represented a very real and effective economy. Attracted by the rapid and noisy passage across the landscape, they even carried a certain tourist trade anxious to experience the satisfactions of narrow gauge even at the risk of some discomfort. The Geese carried parcel freight and the mails as well as paying passengers and did business in everything but tonnage frieght in ore concentrates and stock movements which still went in steam.

Occasionally, a Galloping Goose driven furiously in an effort to keep to schedule down a four per cent grade, got out of hand and imitated its protoype in everything but actual flight. When at last its mad progress left the rails, the entire contrivance disintegrated like a powder mill exploding and a reserve Goose was dispatched to pick up the mails and the maimed from the hillside they occupied. The Galloping Geese inherited most of the thrills of mountain railroading in its most primitive state of development but no fatalities were ever attributed to them.

Both the legend and the fallible reality of the Rio Grande Southern in its lifetime and posthumously attracted the affectionate regard of many men, none more so than David Lavender whose "Bent's Fort" and "The Big Divide" are classics in the bibliography of the Old West. Years after the railroad had become only a memory, he recalled for the authors of this book, some boyhood souvenirs of the great days of Telluride and the narrow gauge.

"Yes," deposed Lavender, "I once did live along the RGS—Rio Grande Southern.

"I was born in Telluride and grew up on a cattle ranch whose shipping point was sixteen or so miles downriver from there—Placerville, where the RGS came corkscrewing from Dallas Divide down Leopard Creek into the San Miguel canyon, lovely with its terraces of deep red sandstone and its leaning evergreens.

"Beyond Dallas Divide at Ridgway—what a fine rampart the San Juans throw up along there!—the RGS had its junction with the Salida narrow-gauge branch of the Denver & Rio Grande Western (if that is the correct corporate designation). No doubt the traffic departments were aware that two distinct railroads operated between Telluride and Salida, but since we did not change cars it seemed to us an unbroken day-long ride—two hundred miles in about twelve hours; 7 AM to 7 PM if I remember the schedule correctly and if the train was on time, which it generally wasn't.

"I was in my teens then. I suppose that is why sense impressions rather than episodes come back most vividly. The smell of coal smoke in red plush.

The flatcar dolled up with railing and seats that was coupled on behind the train as an observation car for the ride through the Black Canyon of the Gunnison: The flanges shrilled between the vast brown walls, the rush of the rapids twined up in a ball of noise with the chuff of the engine—and we *always* got cinders in our eyes. Inside the coaches the oil lamps came on early on winter nights; the shadows leaned as we creaked around the curves —left and back and right and back—and a spot of hot metal glowed in the stove at the end of the aisle and the stale air grew—brassy, is the only word I can think of, and everyone sank farther in his seat, head lolling, not resting, just numb. And then after we pulled off the last hill below Telluride onto the willow flats, speed quickened. Everyone stirred, the click of the rails deepened as the door opened, the conductor bawled his invariable wit, 'To Hell You Ride!' and we knew we were home.

"Dallas Divide, Cerro Summit, and the most ponderous lift of all, Marshall Pass—how the little train roared and belched and shook . . . and crept. The snail's pace gave rise to innumerable bad jokes, endlessly repeated. (Lady to conductor: Can't this train go faster? I'm about to have a baby. Conductor: You shouldn't have gotten on in such condition. Lady: I wasn't in this condition when I got on.)

"Sometimes when there were girls to show off to, the boys would leap from the iron platform of the rear coach, run off to the side, swoop up a wildflower in a handful of grass, and bring it back in panting pride. Occasionally, on suitable stretches, we would run up beside the laboring locomotive and ask the engineer whether we could ride in the cab. It always made the crew furious; the conductor would threaten dire punishments that never materialized. We flattered ourselves that the irritation rose from our lack of respect for their mechanical marvels, not bothering to reflect that even a narrow-gauge wheel could slice an arm or leg off a fallen idiot.

"An easy camaraderie existed between the train crews and the countryside. In those days (the 1920's) and in those mountains, the gasoline buggy was not a serious competitor. Automobile roads were fearful, unpaved and devastated by each rain. I remember several automobiles being stalled by a vanished bridge in the San Miguel canyon. The nearby railroad trestle stood firm, however, and someone suggested laying planks on the open ties and crossing over them. I do not recall where the lumber came from, probably a habitation back down the road a bit, but we all had shovels, for no one dared drive without one. So, we hacked away onto the railroad bed, lined up in automobiles, and began crossing over the flood—gingerly business, for the unrailed trestle edge was scarcely wider than the wheels. Before everyone was over a freight came along, stopped, and politely waited until the last automobile had scuttled back to its own proper habitat.

"Another time, my stepfather's car bogged in a mudhole at a crossing not far from Ridgway. He walked to the roundhouse in town and told his troubles. Down came an engine and pulled him free. Occasionally, the favors could be repaid. Once in the Black Canyon, the male passengers were recruited to help shovel mudslides off the tracks—nine obstructions in twenty miles, as I recall.

"What I remember most were the stock trains, double-headed in front, another engine in the middle, sometimes a pusher behind. The crummy was a bilious apple green. When the train started—what an unearthly running bang as the slack went out of the couplings—the caboose's wild and sudden leap almost snapped your head off.

"We brought the steers out of rough country, down Specie Canyon and up the Miguel to the yards at Placerville, and it was always late when we arrived. The October nights came early and cold. Nothing special ever happened, just prodding the cattle up the chutes into the cars. The slatted fences made long black and yellow patterns under the electric lights on the poles, lanterns waved, the engine *choughed* softly to itself as it waited to pull the next car into place, and somehow the familiar cattle looked all at once strange and eerie as chance gleams of light momentarily turned their eyeballs red or shone on the mist rising from their nostrils. One o'clock, two o'clock—and off to the dining room in Steve Adam's dingy yellow railroad hotel to eat a sodden meal and roll into one of his brass-knobbed beds before going back for another drag.

"Passenger traffic vanished first, of course; then trucks took the cattle and ore. And then the Goose came, that monstrous hybrid of an efficiency expert's mating with a balance sheet. It was high time to tear up the tracks and leave."

Until the very end the motive power roster of the RGS constituted a rare and rewarding museum of atmospheric antiquities, some of them veritable specimens of archeology for the connoisseur of such matters, and several of its more venerable engines were held by local legend to bear the marks of Indian warfare. Consolidations whose capped stacks had been showering the San Juan with cinders before Dewey took Manila bore the insigne of the Rio Grande Southern while outside frame 2-8-2S leased or borrowed from the Denver & Rio Grande Western handled the heavier tonnage on the grades at Dallas, Lizard Head and out of Durango. Photogenic veterans such as No. 20 earned their keep performing in screen Westerns where, with stag's antlers and great oil burning headlights, they recreated a time but slightly antedating their own life span. The last engine to be acquired under the Rio Grande Southern insigne was the Rio Grande's Baldwin-built No. 461, a comparatively powerful 2-8-2 which was purchased in 1950 and later officiated at the obsequies of its final owner.

A cynical observer might be excused for remarking that the entire existence of the Rio Grande Southern has been lived on borrowed time, but the final and most dramatic loan was made when, the merest chance of pre-Jurassic geology decreed that mineral deposits along the San Miguel River were rich with Carnotite and its vanadium derivitive known as "red cake." A by-product of vanadium manufacture is another something called "yellow cake" which had so little commercial value that for years it was thrown out on the tailing dumps along the San Miguel and washed away when the river flooded, which was fairly often. At least, uranium oxide was valueless until Albert Einstein wrote a letter to President Roosevelt. Suddenly an entire region of which the faltering Rio Grande Southern Railroad was the nerve center, became the most jealously guarded mineral deposit in the world and Federal agents were riding the tops of ore cars carrying cargoes that only yesterday vanadium mill owners were throwing out the window. Strangers around Placerville and Telluride had to explain their business; a loan from the Reconstruction Finance Corporation bolstered the railroad's tottering economy, and the leased Rio Grande locomotives hauling machine-gun-guarded high cars over Dallas Divide had an ultimate destination, although nobody at the moment knew it, at Hiroshima.

It was the final irony of fate that the railroad that was packing its cylinder valves with old shirting and, figuratively, didn't know where its next meal was coming from, should suddenly, and because no other means of transport existed in the region, be carrying the hottest freight in the long history of railroad operations.

In December 1951 as the storm clouds of winter were gathering over Trout Lake and the trestles at Ophir were assuming a Christmas card appearance under the first snowfall, time had done with the Rio Grande Southern Railroad. Three years earlier the mines in Rico and Telluride had turned to trucks and, at one blow, eliminated nearly seventy per cent of the carrier's gross revenue. A $30,000 mail contract had been canceled by the Post Office after residents at one-line stops who had lived on the railroad's bounty for sixty years complained, ungrateful as peasants always, that the Galloping Goose was late with their Sears Roebuck catalogues.

The railroad's chronic insolvency reached a climax and its obligations, totaling $9,045,407.47 on September 30, 1951 have been tabulated by Robert Richardson as follows:

Bonds, $4,509,000.00
  5,669,270.00 interest on these bonds, in default
  50,000.00 R.F.C. loan
  634,621.00 "Payable to affiliated company"
    (the D&RGW)
  794,571.17 current liabilities, which included
    $352,000 in accts. & wages payable,
    $312,000 due counties on taxes,
    $40,000 unemployment taxes,
    $83,000 railroad retirement payments.

In the face of an $8,000 monthly operating deficit, the road's final receiver, Pierpont Fuller, Jr., decided to put up the shutters. To the last the RGS was crotchety and reluctant to abide by the decisions of mere men. On its last cleanup train, the Denver & Rio Grande Western's Mikado No. 452, sent by the parent company to pick up the pieces, set its tender on the ground at Vance Junction while running as helper south out of Ridgway. At Rico, on Thanksgiving eve, the crew of No. 461, the Southern's most modern and powerful 2-8-2, spotted it for the night and went to town for turkey dinner. During the dark hours the temperature plunged to ten below and condensed steam and boiler leakage from the engine froze its trucks and drivers in insoluble bondage to the roadbed. All along the way engine crews had to buck snowdrifts, nurse balky injectors, run for water and generally nurse the invalid through its terminal illness.

Terrible tempered, like its builder Otto Mears, to the end the improbable Rio Grande Southern nevertheless confounded prophets of doom for decades and outlived many a more robust and promising contemporary. The Friar Lawrence of the narrow gauges, its entire life span a record of confusion and mistaken missions, it left its impress on the elemental Colorado earth and in the memory of two entire generations of the American West. In the roundhouse of eternity there are neither derailments nor creditors and its rest is untroubled in the surrounding night.

WESTERN COLLECTION

OTTO PERRY

WESTERN COLLECTION

DURANGO HERALD NEWS

Never one to neglect the uses of publicity where his properties were concerned, Otto Mears took a leaf out of General Palmer's book and retained the services of the foremost photographer of the time and place to publicize the scenic wonderments along the route of the Rio Grande Southern. William H. Jackson was provided with the two ornate business cars depicted above, the *Rico* and No. 1, and the road's No. 1, paused for their portrait at Lizard Head in the spring of 1895. BELOW: the interior of a similarly rococo business car of the period, General Palmer's *Nomad*. Behind the Pintsch light is a sign, perhaps the inspiration of a later day, reading "Please Do Not Shoot Buffalo From the Train." On the page opposite, the station agent at Placerville and his wife pose for the cameraman in the same year, while BELOW nearly half a century later, RGS No. 42, carrying white at its smoke box, runs as helper to No. 40 as road engine with a stock extra up the ruling grade at Dallas Divide in October, 1940.

203

Two miles up-canyon from the Southern's depot at Ophir, there once flourished the mining community of Old Ophir whence two carloads of concentrates were shipped daily, year in and year out, to go out by Mears' narrow gauge from the loading tipple shown here. In 1898 Old Ophir had waterworks, electric lights and a population of 400 whose social life centered around the well-patronized Colorado House. Today grass grows in the streets of Old Ophir and sheep graze on once well-kept lawns. The long night claimed the mines first, then the town and at last the railroad.

CHARLES CLEGG

RICHARD KINDIG

WESTERN COLLECTION

The extremely rare photograph ABOVE, exhumed from deposits of geological antiquity in the Denver Library, shows a D&RG narrow gauge diner specially assigned to the Narrow Gauge Circle excursion traffic as it paused for luncheon overlooking picturesque Trout Lake, the flowers and snowy nappery visible through its windows as testimony to the niceties of travel at the time. BELOW is Trout Lake. On the page opposite, RGS No. 74 poses for its portrait on the Ophir Trestle and Ophir depot basks in the autumn sun, behind it the ore chutes through which, in times of teem, poured millions in precious metals to the waiting cars.

OTTO PERRY

On the page opposite, a view looking down over the fabled high trestle at Ophir suggests why Otto Mears, when first confronted with this engineering masterpiece, got down from his business car and walked across, while BELOW, a CCC special in the year 1940 heads out onto the span with No. 22 as helper and Rio Grande No. 453 as road engine. On this page, No. 20 pauses for a drink at the track-side water tower at Mancos while in the lower frame, No. 461 scurries out of Rico with a consist of ore cars bound for the high pass at Lizard Head and an eventual connection with the Denver & Rio Grande Western at Ridgway. The year is 1947, and time is running out for the last of Otto Mears's narrow gauges.

CHARLES CLEGG

EDGAR T. MEADE, JR.

TWO PHOTOS: OTTO PERRY

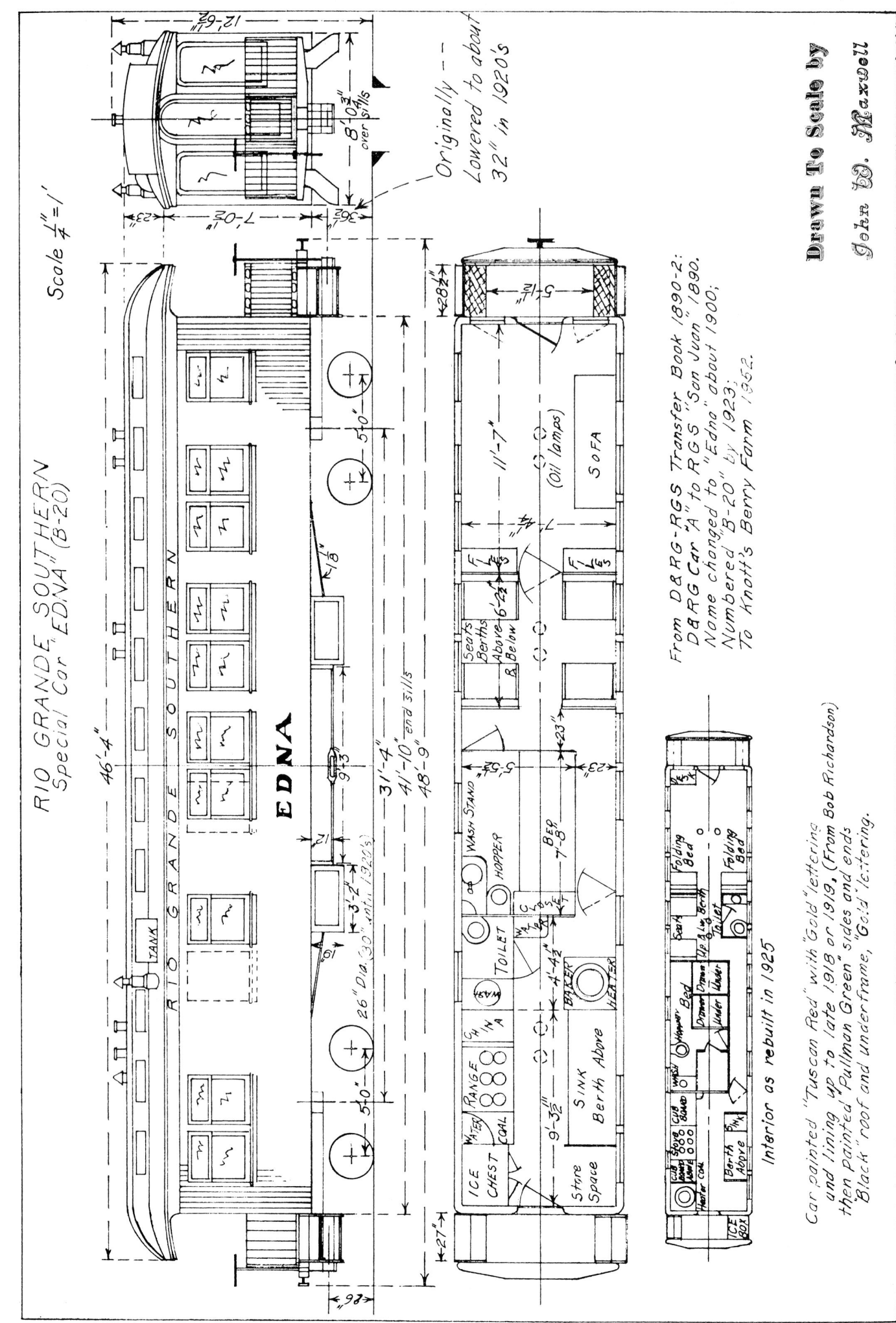

COLORADO STATE HISTORICAL SOCIETY

No short line in history had more special equipment and business cars in proportion to its operations than the Rio Grande Southern in its heyday. ABOVE: R.G.S. No. 9 poses for its portrait with the business car *Rico*, against a backdrop of distant Lizard Head, while BELOW, in the year 1895, a special train, probably for the entertainment of Otto Mears's guests, follows a double-headed freight around the loop at Mancos-La Plata Divide with the Mancos Creek tank in the foreground. Both photographs were by the peerless William H. Jackson. On the page opposite are blueprints for the RGS business car, *Edna*.

RICHARD KINDIG COLLECTION

Delighted with the prestige that had accrued to his Silverton Railroad with its stylish hotel car, *Animas Forks,* Otto Mears for a number of years scheduled Pullman sleepers on the overnight run on the Rio Grande Southern between Ridgway and Durango. Here, in keeping with Palmer's law of no more than one sleeper to a berth, mine superintendents bound for Rico and cattle buyers ticketed to Mancos slept snugly, while blizzards raged in the night outside and the little cars swayed perilously across the trestles of Ophir and over the divide at Lizard Head. In the below photograph, the Southern's sleepers are shown being pressed into service for a gala outing of the Sky City Miner's Club of Red Mountain and Mine Superintendents of Telluride, combined, a short distance above Vance Junction on the Telluride branch of the narrow gauge.

JACK THODE COLLECTION

CHARLES CLEGG

LUCIUS BEEBE

In 1945, as time was running out for the RGS, the authors of this volume were the guests of General Manager of the D&RGW, A. E. Perlman, aboard the business cars B-2 and B-7 for what was probably the last passenger run in steam over what remained of the Narrow Gauge Circle. The office cars were cut into the then running *San Juan* at Alamosa, and from Durango to Ridgway ran in mixed freight as shown above, for a final tour of Otto Mears's railroad, including the Telluride branch. BELOW: B-2 and B-7 are shown paused briefly at Hesperus.

WALKER ART STUDIOS, MONTROSE

RICHARD B. JACKSON

JAMES M. MORLEY

In Pandora Basin, past the Telluride cemetery and the ruins of the Liberty Bell Mine, the tracks of the RGS led to Pandora and the Smuggler Union Mine, scene of fantastic recoveries in Telluride's heyday. Here spring flowers bloom between the rails where once the engines ran for a Pandora pastoral, while beyond the rustic fence can be seen the new line of track leading to the box canyon where the Black Bear Mine was located below Ingram Falls. PAGE OPPOSITE: When a spring freshet washed out the RGS tracks to Telluride many years ago, the camp's tremendous thirst was temporarily slacked by the heroic expedient of packing beer in from Vance Junction by mule brigade, and the arrangement was known as the Budweiser Relief Train. The washed-out rails are visible at the left. BELOW: No. 22 edges gingerly out onto Lightner Trestle just west of Durango with a merchandise consist for Dolores prominent, in which are two cars of Conoco products.

JACKSON THODE COLLECTION

When snows became too deep on Dallas Divide, the RGS borrowed a rotary from the Rio Grande, as shown above. Ordinary winter conditions could be coped with by the company's own plow and flanger, shown in 1912 at Ridgway, with its designer and builder, Andrew Rassmussen.

WESTERN COLLECTION

JOHNNY KRAUSE

Where once the narrow gauge business cars cars of Otto Mears and later the Galloping Goose ran in the shadow of Ophir Needles, a Rio Grande Southern Clean-up train operated by the dismantlers with an extra water tender behind 451 moves upgrade above Ophir Depot. The rugged background is typical at once of the grandeur of the Colorado landscape and the geography with which Otto Mears contended.

LUCIUS BEEBE

In the meadows of Mancos, the head shack of a Rio Grande Southern freight in the last years of its lonely operations opens a switch to set out a cut of stock cars for a local shipper in this rich grazing district.

"Here She Comes, There She Goes," is the title given to these two superlative photographs of the Rio Grande Southern's No. 455, by photographer Richard B. Jackson near the summit at Dallas Divide in 1941. As the camera turned with the train's passing to catch the caboose, it also embraced a distant vista of Mt. Sneffels in the snowy Uncompaghres.

TWO PHOTOS: RICHARD B. JACKSON

EDGAR T. MEADE, JR.

RICHARD B. JACKSON

JAMES R. JACKSON

Over the Fourth of July, in 1938, Victor Miller, receiver for the Rio Grande Southern, was host to John Barriger, then president of the Monon Railroad in Indiana, and to honor his guest, Miller ordered a special train to make the run over the entire mileage of the loneliest and most picturesque of narrow gauges. To lend solidity to the consist, a coach was hitched to the drawbar of No. 25 and the party entrained aboard the road's last remaining business car behind. On the page opposite, the special is shown on the long, curved trestle at Lightner Creek a couple of miles west of Durango, while ABOVE, the deserted depot but still activated water tower at Ophir Springs awaits the daily arrival of the Galloping Goose or a less frequent freight. On this page, No. 25 rolls up Dallas Divide with one more special in the long tally of RGS excursions over the Colorado years.

JAMES M. MORLEY

In July, 1941, northbound Goose No. 7 went into the hole for two southbound Geese loaded with CCC personnel in a grassy valley south of Ridgway. The meet turned into a minor social event and some of the boys posed for this expressive photograph by Jim Morley. Whether it was its wildly improbable name or valiant enlistment in a lost cause that attracted sympathetic attention, the Galloping Goose became, in its lifetime a Colorado institution of the first magnitude.

OTTO PERRY

No. 5 Goose pauses at the depot platform at Placerville beside the San Miguel River to set out the mail and local freight and passengers on a summer's morning in 1940.

This official inspection car of the Rio Grande Southern rebuilt from a Model-T Ford was designed by Superintendent of Motive Power W. D. Lee, shown in the photo at the left with his dream bus. At the bottom of the page a Rio Grande Southern Galloping Goose of somewhat more sophisticated design pauses briefly in 1945 as the driver sets out the mail at an obscure tank-stop on the run between Dolores and Ophir.

WESTERN COLLECTION

CHARLES CLEGG

In July, 1935, as history was moving toward a climactic moment in the annals of the Rio Grande Southern in the form of the Manhattan Project and a bomb over Hiroshima, this double-headed freight approaching Lizard Head snowsheds behind engines No. 42 and 40 provided a matchless subject for the camera of Richard Jackson.

RICHARD B. JACKSON